Finally ME

Testimonials

"Frank Sala shares a heartfelt journey of Awakening. Told through honest words and magnificent illustration, Sala shares his travels—with the help of healers and guides—from inner isolation and despair to discover through his augmented perception the deeper unitive reality: the sacred interconnected, oneness. We discover with Sala, that as we Awaken, we see that we are in the loving company of all life: trees, wolves, ancestors and spirits. Back to living in our birthright of Eden we again perceive the truth: that we are loved, guided and never alone."

—Lisa Miller, Ph.D., Bestselling Author of *The Awakened Brain: The New Science of Spirituality and Our Quest for an Inspired Life*

"A profound manual for healing the emotional and physical body. *Finally ME* offers deep wisdom about the nature of the healing journey—how trauma fragments us and how we can reclaim lost parts of ourselves. I found myself reflecting on my own life, my own pain, and my own untapped strength. This book will change lives."

—Susan Lambert, M.D.

"*Finally ME* offers an intimate, heartfelt look at the healing power of shamanic counseling. Frank's story isn't just about facing trauma; it's about rediscovering the artist within. Valerie's support is both deeply compassionate and genuinely life changing. This book is a beautiful reminder of how resilient we really are, and how powerful alternative healing can be."

—Rachael Jayne Groover, Best-selling author of *Unshakable Inner Peace*, and *Founder of The Awakened School*

"*Finally ME* is a moving account of healing and transformation. Frank's courage in sharing his journey is inspirational. The skill and compassion with which Valerie guides him through the shamanic process reveals the incredible potential we each have to reclaim our lives from debilitating trauma. This book is a testament to the resilience of the human spirit and the life-changing potential of integrative healing practices that recognize the profound connection between body, mind and spirit. Congratulations on this powerful collaboration."

—Ellen F. Franklin, Ph.D., Co-Author of *Acutonics® from Galaxies to Cells: Planetary Science, Harmony & Medicine*

—Donna Carey, LAc, Co-Author of *Acutonics There's No Place Like Ohm* and *Acutonics® from Galaxies to Cells: Planetary Science, Harmony & Medicine*, and the poetry collection: *Dreaming with Elk*

"Valerie Devi Carpenter is a brilliant healer who genuinely cares about others. Her passion and deep understanding of the healing journey come through on every page of this book. What I loved most is how effortlessly it delivers powerful lessons—you're learning without even realizing it. Through Valerie's guidance, Frank not only reclaims his life but also uncovers his soul's true purpose. It's an easy, inspiring read for anyone looking for real transformation."

—Del Lewis, CEO, and Bestselling Author of *Get Your Ship Together*

Finally ME

How Shamanic Journeying Healed Childhood Trauma and Gave Me Back My Life

FRANK SALA and VALERIE DEVI CARPENTER

FINALLY ME

Illustrations by Frank Sala, CoAuthored and Edited by Valerie Devi Carpenter
Publishing Services provided by Stacey Smekofske @ Print To Pro
Book Design by Tara Mayberry @ TeaBerryStudio.com

Published by Sound Living Wisdom

The author has attempted to recreate events, locales, and conversations from memory.

This publication is meant as a source of valuable information for the reader; however, it is not meant as a substitute for direct expert assistance. If such a level of assistance is required, the services of a competent professional should be sought.

If you are in crisis or need immediate support, please contact the Suicide & Crisis Lifeline by calling or texting 988 (US) or reach out to a local mental health service in your area. Help is available.

For permission requests, write the publisher at valerie@soundliving.com

Library of Congress Control Number: 2025920168
Hardcover: 979-8-9902547-0-1
Paperback: 979-8-9902547-1-8
eBook: 979-8-9902547-2-5

Dedicated to Meg Sala-James
and Robert James,
whose kindness provided me
with a home in which
the following story took place.

INTO THE UNKNOWN

by Valerie Devi Carpenter

Healing is a journey—one that takes courage, curiosity, and a willingness to step into the unknown. In these pages, you'll witness a remarkable transformation as Frank takes that leap, guided by the beat of the shaman's drum, spirit allies, and the healing power of creativity.

Frank's story is one of resilience, self-discovery, and ultimately, reclamation. When we first began working together, he was searching for something—though he couldn't quite name it. Like so many of us, he had spent years trying to mend the fractures of his past through therapy, self-help, and sheer determination. But deep healing doesn't come from willpower alone. It requires something more—something ancient, intuitive, and deeply personal.

For three years, Frank and I explored these hidden realms together. Through sound, stillness, and the rhythmic pulse of the drum, he learned to access the vast inner landscape of his own being—a space where wisdom, healing, and lost parts of his self awaited him. This process, known as Shamanic Counseling, isn't about being given answers. It's about learning to listen—to symbols, sensations, and the language of the soul. My role was to offer guidance, helping Frank interpret the visions and insights that surfaced in his Sacred Garden—a place in the spirit world where healing unfolds.

This work is deeply rooted in the teachings of my own mentors, Hank Wesselman and Jill Kuykendall, whose wisdom shaped both my practice and this book. The act of journeying—of meeting spirit helpers, reclaiming lost parts of ourselves, and weaving those experiences into daily life—is as old as humanity itself. But Frank brought something truly unique to the process: his art.

At first, he sketched simply to document what he saw. But soon, his drawings became something more: a bridge between worlds, a visual language for healing. With each journey, his illustrations gave form to the emotions, insights, and breakthroughs that words alone couldn't fully capture. What you'll find in these pages is more than a memoir. It's a map of a soul's return home.

As you read Frank's story, I invite you to reflect on your own. Healing isn't reserved for the chosen few. The same unseen world that guided Frank is available to you. His journey is an invitation to look within, to listen deeply, and to step toward the wholeness that has always been yours.

I dedicate this book to Hank and Jill, who now walk in the realm of the Ancestors, continuing to light the way for all of us who seek.

With love and deep gratitude,

Valerie Devi Carpenter

Valerie Devi Sound Living

MY UNHAPPY LIFE

It sucked to be me.

I am not having a pity party. This was just a fact, and this is why: I never felt the sum of my parts. Not that I didn't try.

After decades of cognitive therapy, self-help books, inspirational seminars, and serious religious pursuits, I could accurately describe the mechanics of my emotional dysfunction and even list several likely DMS-5 diagnoses. Sadly, knowledge of my malady did not mend my dismal, unhappy life.

As I struggled in life, time passed. I watched as people found friendship and romantic love that grew deeper with time. For me, time was an enemy. My friendships and romances all had very short lives.

In my early 40s, I concluded that my ability to participate in my own life—something that appeared to be abundantly available to others—would always elude me. I settled for a dystopic life of complete self-abnegation. It was my choice—the only one I saw.

I was a burglar in my own body. A trespasser. An impostor.

Then, at 60, I met someone.

She offered to help me build a Garden. She said this Garden would bring healing. I accepted her help, and why not?

My lifelong pursuit to find wholeness had only left me sad and alone. And, after losing my youth, my loves, my career, my dignity, and my family standing, I had nothing left to lose.

Mind you, this is not a love story. It is a true story about healing. You see, this woman, Valerie, is a Master Gardener, and she also works with me as a mentor, healer, and guide. Let me explain.

The Garden I speak of is not made of soil and water. This Garden is made from compassion and strength, power, and knowledge. It is my Sacred Garden, and it is found in the realm of non-ordinary experience.

Sacred Gardens are not governed by the rules of time and space. Rather, four principles shape each Garden, as follows:

1. Everything in your Garden is symbolic of something in your life.
2. You can communicate with anyone or anything in your Garden.
3. You can plant, build and arrange the Garden as you wish, and...
4. Any change you make in your Garden will change something in your ordinary reality.

My Sacred Garden is quite populated. Its inhabitants include kittens, a wolf, an enormous wise tree, and a multitude of spirits.

Valerie taught me how to discover my Garden and helped me learn how to tend it. She learned how from her teacher Hank, an anthropologist and spiritual visionary, who was introduced to the process by his teacher, another anthropologist named Michael. I learned that this path—the path of the shaman—is as old as human history.

The practice used to walk this path, which is accessible to anyone, is called "shamanic journeying," an ancient practice completely new to this Italian-American Baby Boomer born and bred in the suburbs of Long Island, New York.

To avoid confusion, from now on I will refer to Valerie—who, in ordinary reality, actually lives three time zones away from me—as Coach.

CHAPTER ONE

A HELPER FOR MY JOURNEYS

During my first session, the only one I got to do in person, Coach asked me to lie on my back and close my eyes.

"How does your body feel?" she asked.

"Tense," I replied. It was an understatement. I had a tight gut. Tense arms and legs. My brow was furrowed like corn rows.

"Pay attention to how you are breathing. Tell me what you notice," she requested.

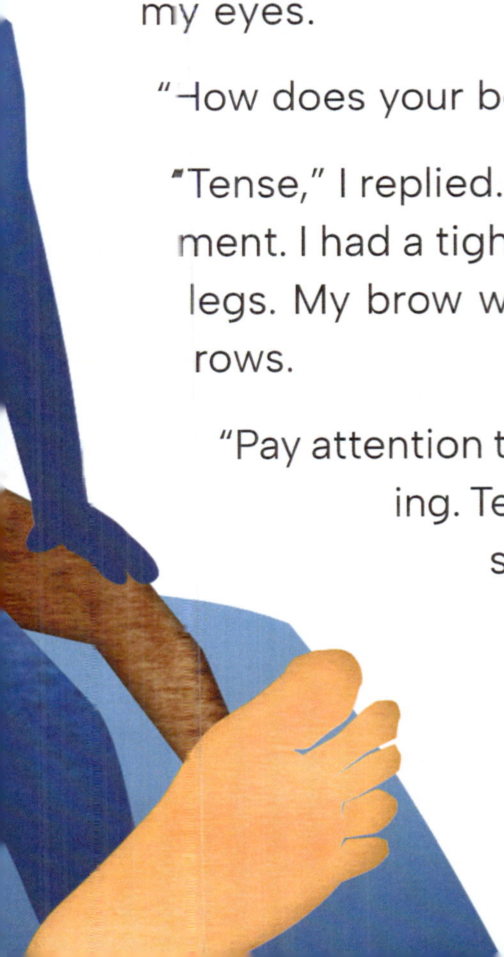

To my surprise, I realized my breath was barely more than a tiny whiff of air being pulled in and out from high in my chest. It was so shallow that my chest hardly moved up and down. Then I noticed that my diaphragm was firmly cemented to my gut, rendering it nearly immobile. That's when she taught me how to breathe.

"Follow the breath," she said. "First, fill your belly. Allow the lower belly to expand and release with the breath. Now allow your breath to fill the lower part of your ribcage, so the ribcage expands and contracts with the breath.

"Remember that your ribs go all the way around—there's a lot more space available than you think." She counted slow beats to inhale and exhale.

I obliged. It seemed harmless, and I did not mind the attention.

Gradually, my body began to relax and settle into the cushions. Rest was enough for me. I was not expecting anything more. But shortly thereafter, I sensed Coach was doing...something. I stirred.

"Relax and keep your eyes closed," she responded. "Breathe slowly and deeply." There was a bit more movement.

Then stillness.

The silence was broken by a strange chant-like incantation that seemed to last forever, as if time stopped and I was suspended in Sound.

Coach's voice was beautiful as it traced out a melody that was impossible to follow. Short notes turned into long wails only to morph into a gibberish that varied from a yell to a whisper and back, evoking a

dim glow of memories, associations and emotions far below the surface.

Then, Coach fell silent. I waited—mildly startled, entranced, and just a bit curious.

I remained on my back with my eyes closed—still the self-hating burglar trapped in a body. And though I yearned for healing at age 60, I expected nothing.

We remained in silence for a few minutes and then she spoke.

"Someone wants to meet you." she said.

"Okay," I replied, playing along.

"Shhh," Coach gently urged. "You don't need to talk. Stay in the moment. Stay in the quiet state you have entered." She remained silent for a few moments for me to settle back before continuing.

"There is a Spirit Helper who wants to meet you," she said. "May I introduce you by breathing this Spirit into your heart and then the crown of your head?"

"In for a penny..." I thought and nodded. She breathed.

"It's a wolf. A white wolf. Can you sense it?"

"No." I replied after a moment. I propped up my body on an elbow and turned to look at her.

"Keep your eyes closed," she said, gently moving my shoulder back down to the cushion.

"This wolf is a spirit that will restore your strength and courage so you can find the healing you have asked for. It is a Spirit Helper who will give you power, protection, and support," she said.

This time, I listened with some intrigue.

She continued. "I did not choose this particular helper. I simply put out a call for a spirit to answer your need. Spirit Helpers respond to those who seek help honestly, innocently, openly."

I fit that bill. That day I lay there empty, consumed by decades of confusion, anger, jealousy, and self-pity. Self-loathing. Still trapped in a body after a long, lonely lifetime, I only wanted to heal and knew I needed help.

It was then that I sensed him. Somehow, I could tell he was male. Silent of words, but clear on intent, I could also sense that he was present solely to stand by my side. He was fully committed to me in a manner that was curiously emotionally unadorned. He was not a friend, nor a tutor, and certainly not an affectionately nuzzling canine pet! Rather, he seemed to be a comrade-in-arms. A strong fellow soldier, not a leader or a sergeant. Perhaps a muscular medic.

Slowly, an image formed behind my closed eyes.

A wolf. Sturdy. Strong. Thick fur. White, but not pure white. It was mixed with gray. Powerful muscles defined his back and limbs. His eyes held a steady, calm gaze that told me he was ready.

Ready?

Ready for what? I wondered. I hadn't a clue. Coach continued her instruction.

"If you choose, this Spirit Helper will accompany you on the journeys you will learn to take in non-ordinary reality and walk with you in ordinary, everyday life.

"So, does your white wolf have a name?" she asked.

No name seemed appropriate. I decided to call him White Wolf.

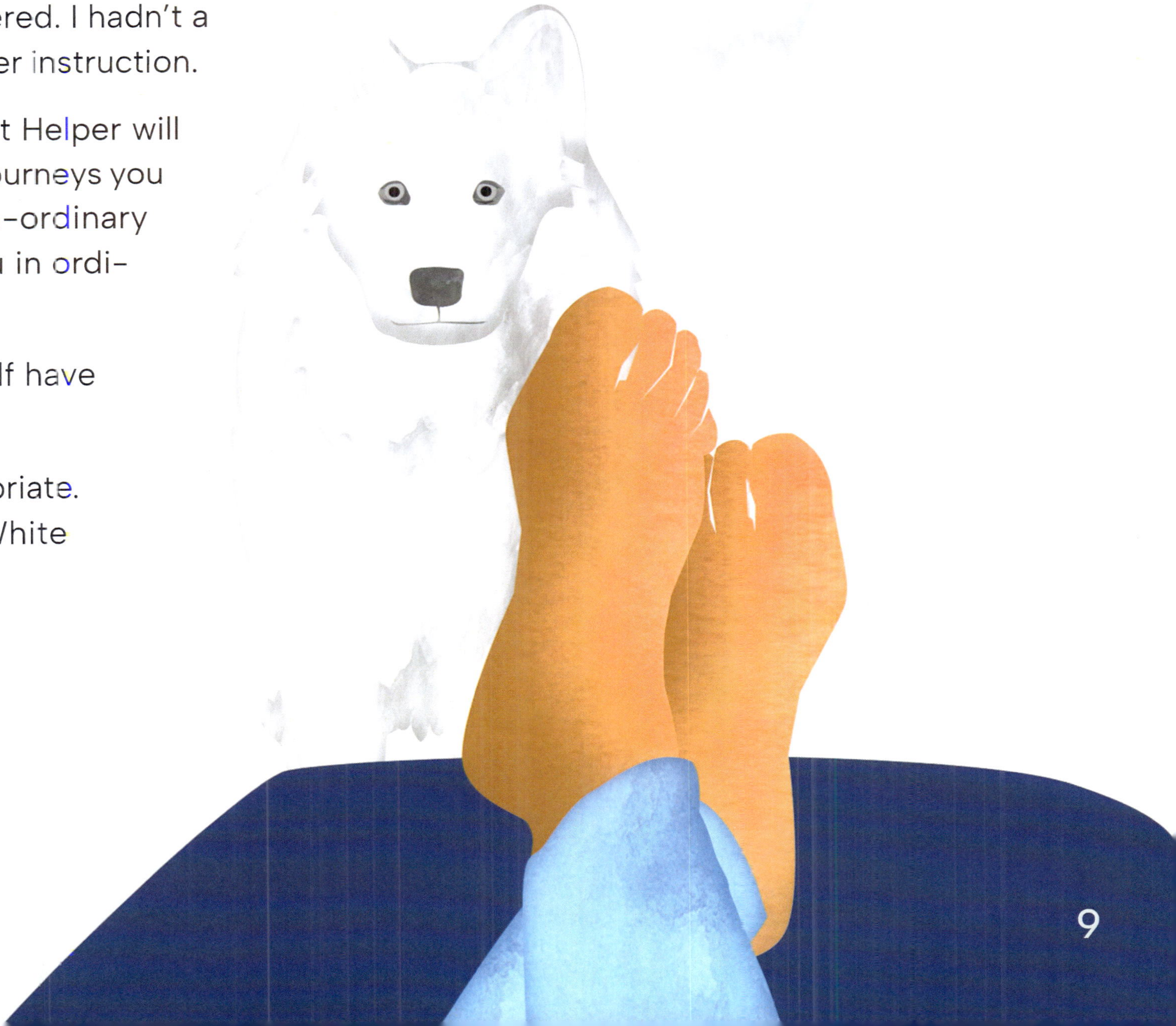

CHAPTER TWO

NOT WHAT I EXPECTED

Coach returned to her home in California, leaving me with my new companion, White Wolf. Day after day, he did not change. He was always present when I noticed him, always a silent comrade. Always "ready" to assist, whatever that meant.

My access to Coach now rested on my desk. A computer screen that hosted weekly video conference sessions. It felt awkward to me in those pre-pandemic days, but to my surprise, the content of the sessions quickly made the technology unnoticeable. I began to appreciate both the intimacy and safety of the container we created using this strange new interface in the comfort of my home.

So, I sat before the screen—a sprawling concoction of misconceptions and self-contempt attempting to understand life and survive each day, having anxiety and depression as my only steppingstones.

Before guiding me on my first journey, Coach addressed the din in my head by making me more aware of the connection between my mind and my body with various breathing and humming techniques. I learned that relaxing my body calmed my mind.

Come the day of my first journey into non-ordinary reality—Whoa! I lay on my bed, the computer monitor glowing softly in the darkened room. Headphones on, I listened while Coach played a steady rhythm on a frame drum. She asked me to set a strong intention to journey to my "Sacred Garden"—whatever that was.

"Frank," she murmured, "I want you to look for some kind of portal, an entrance. It may look like an actual door, a curtain, or a circle of light. It doesn't matter, just pass through it. This portal will be the opening to your Sacred Garden.

"Now call White Wolf to your side for courage." To my amazement, White Wolf appeared beneath my right hand. I felt his deep, lush fur and buried my fingers into his cushy warmth. Again, I sensed he was 'Ready.'

So that's what he meant!

With my arm around him, we dove head-first into black empty space as if diving into water. Ahead was a circle of light, about the size of my body. We glided through the circle and rose to the surface of the black empty space.

This must be it!
The portal to my
Sacred Garden!

I remembered Coach telling me that my Garden didn't need to be an actual garden, but any place that felt like a safe and welcoming refuge.

I looked eagerly around the void. I wanted my Garden to be in another galaxy, far away from my disappointing life. I imagined a galaxy hidden deep within the vastness of the universe, millions of light years far from the spiral we call the Milky Way Galaxy containing a tiny yellow splotch around which planet Earth circles without purpose or destination.

For a luxurious moment, I was free from the confines of my troubled life. I was wonderfully anonymous in the inky blackness of space, the universe sprawled before me. So, imagine my surprise when I...

...was in Dix Hills, New York. HUH? I looked around at the strawberry patch in front of me. It was my...grandpa's! Although it was a little disappointing to find myself back in the middle of nowhere...on Long Island (of all places)... rather than traversing far galaxies in outer space, his garden had been one of my favorite childhood spots.

As I looked around, I noticed, over my left shoulder, a herd of kittens marching straight toward me.

Odd. Grandpa had no cats.

Peculiarly, the kittens arrayed themselves on either side of me, in a quiet orderly fashion. Odder still, they seemed to know me.

"Okaaaaay..." I thought. "Let's see if I can create a garden out of this."

So, I imagined a paint brush. And I traced circles before me, treating the air like a canvas. The kittens watched as swirls of color danced in the air. They were pretty.

And pretty inconsequential, considering the troubles that had brought me here in the first place. Disappointing, yup.

My thoughts returned to building a Sacred Garden in—sigh—Dix Hills, when I noticed a short strand of steppingstones.

They curved just beyond my sight.

Intrigued, I picked up a kitten, held it for courage, and followed the path.

The path led to a warm sandy desert...

...where I felt wonderfully alone and safe.
Blissfully distant, even from time.

Freed from my burgled body.

Maybe I could build my Garden here, I thought to myself. Coach had only instructed me to find a safe place to have the Garden, but I saw no harm in getting to work. A brilliant sun shone on me as I lay down a garden floor of dark and light gray rectangular stones. At the center of the floor, I placed a shallow, round, reflecting pond. The blue sky danced on its surface. Beautiful!

I felt at peace. Calm. I brought in a few songbirds. They flew about briefly.

It was all very nice.

I looked forward to visiting this garden again and again...

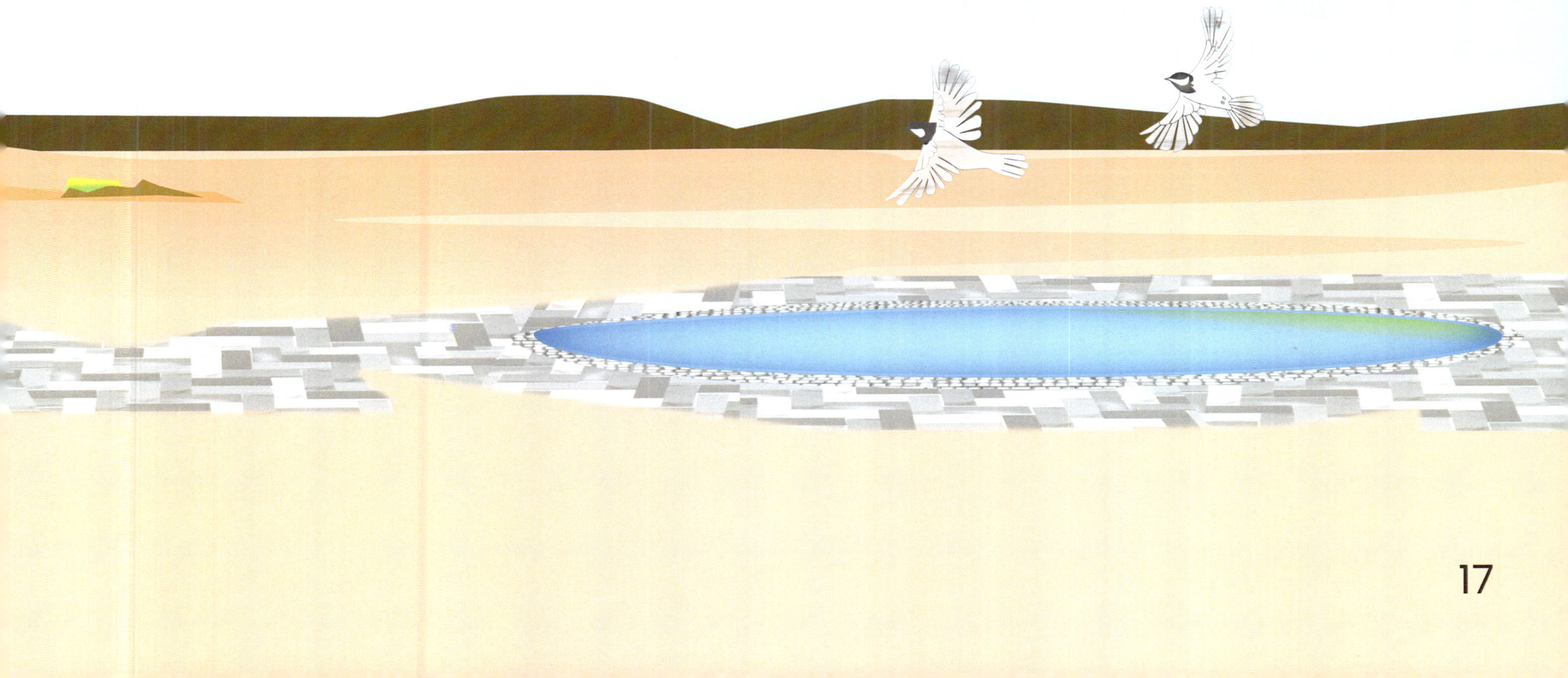

But...

One day—without warning—a journey took me from the desert to a darkened room in my old childhood house.

I found myself as a child, reliving a forgotten memory.

Vivid and dark.

Troubling and true.

It doesn't matter what it was.

It was traumatic.

A shattered trust.

I examined each shard.

Their terrible edges
reflected scars in
my heart and mind,
scars I had carried
throughout life.

And then,

just as suddenly...

...I was back in the desert garden.

The once lovely reflecting pool had turned into a deadened pit.

I saw no flame, only a billowing column of sooty, black smoke.

Smoldering at its base was something foul. Something repugnant. But the fire was slow and controlled. It seemed all-consuming and somehow cleansing.

I searched myself for foul things to be rid of to throw into the pit. I don't know what I grabbed, but I watched as everything I tossed in smoldered, adding to the column of smoke.

I had questions.

Was this my own shame? Anger? Rage? Could old smelly emotions have stopped me from being able to participate in my own life? How? And what of those emotions?

Could I be rid of them?

With questions unanswered, I returned to the portal and back into ordinary reality, stepping into my daily life.

I knew it was time to
confer with Coach.

Feeling dis-"spirited," I shared with Coach the trauma I had relived. It was easy to describe the details, but very difficult to understand my feelings about the ordeal in the present, ordinary reality.

"I distinctly remember my confusion, the sense of betrayal and the great shame that I felt as a child—as if it had just happened. But I do not know what to do with those feelings," I said. "Those feelings are huge. Worse, I'm starting to think those feelings may have impacted my reactions, decisions, and general performance in life."

"General performance?" Coach echoed, sensing my harsh self-judgment. I stood ready to catalog and defend my failures. But rather than challenge my self-estimation, Coach became an advocate for my broken heart.

"You've been through a lot. You're holding a lot of pain. The pain from your trauma is real. The pain, however, can also be a source of great strength if it is embraced.

"For your next journey, I want you to clarify your intention to find a place in the spirit world that brings you comfort, a refuge for safety and healing. If you find yourself again reliving any trauma, don't dwell on the details. Instead, get curious about the feelings that come up and call on White Wolf for protection and support. In time, you will learn to navigate this new terrain, but let's start with the concept of 'safety first.'"

I listened to her, hoping to understand. When I realized I could not, I simply took her at her word. Then she surprised me with three specific instructions.

"First, I want you to go back to those steppingstones near your grandfather's strawberry patch and see if you can find a garden gate.

"Next, see if there's a tree.

And finally, Frank, try to have a little fun."

I thought.

CHAPTER THREE

LOOKING FOR A TREE

On my next journey, I found that the desert garden and firepit were gone. A strange murky haze blocked my view.

Coach had said to look for a garden gate. When I tried to visualize what the gate might look like, dozens of different gates flickered before my eyes.

It made me dizzy.

Eventually, I gave up and decided to focus on finding the tree Coach mentioned. I figured it would be one of my favorite trees.

A white birch? A willow?

I could not decide and did not know how I could find that tree.

Back in ordinary reality, I asked Coach for further instructions.

"How do I find that tree?" I asked. "I picture a tree in my head, but that's as far as I get."

"Don't *look for* the tree," Coach offered "Try to sense it. Listen for it with an open mind and an inward ear. Ask the tree to call to you."

On my next journey, I found myself still surrounded by the murky haze.

So, I relaxed, closed my eyes, and asked for the tree to greet me. After a short while, I sensed I was not alone. At first, I felt a gentle presence, like a breeze. Then a whisper.

Then a soft voice.

A form came into view, slowly, like when your eyes adjust to a new level of light.

I watched as the form became clearer and broader. Taller. It continued to grow until what stood before me was...

magnificent!

Before me stood an enormous tree!

Flaring roots somehow held its base firmly to the hazy ground. Its massive trunk rose far above my head before dividing into several primary branches. Each was like a majestic arm covered in bark comprised of countless pages. The pages held a story, but I could not read what was written. Those tremendous arms carried the pages up and out of sight.

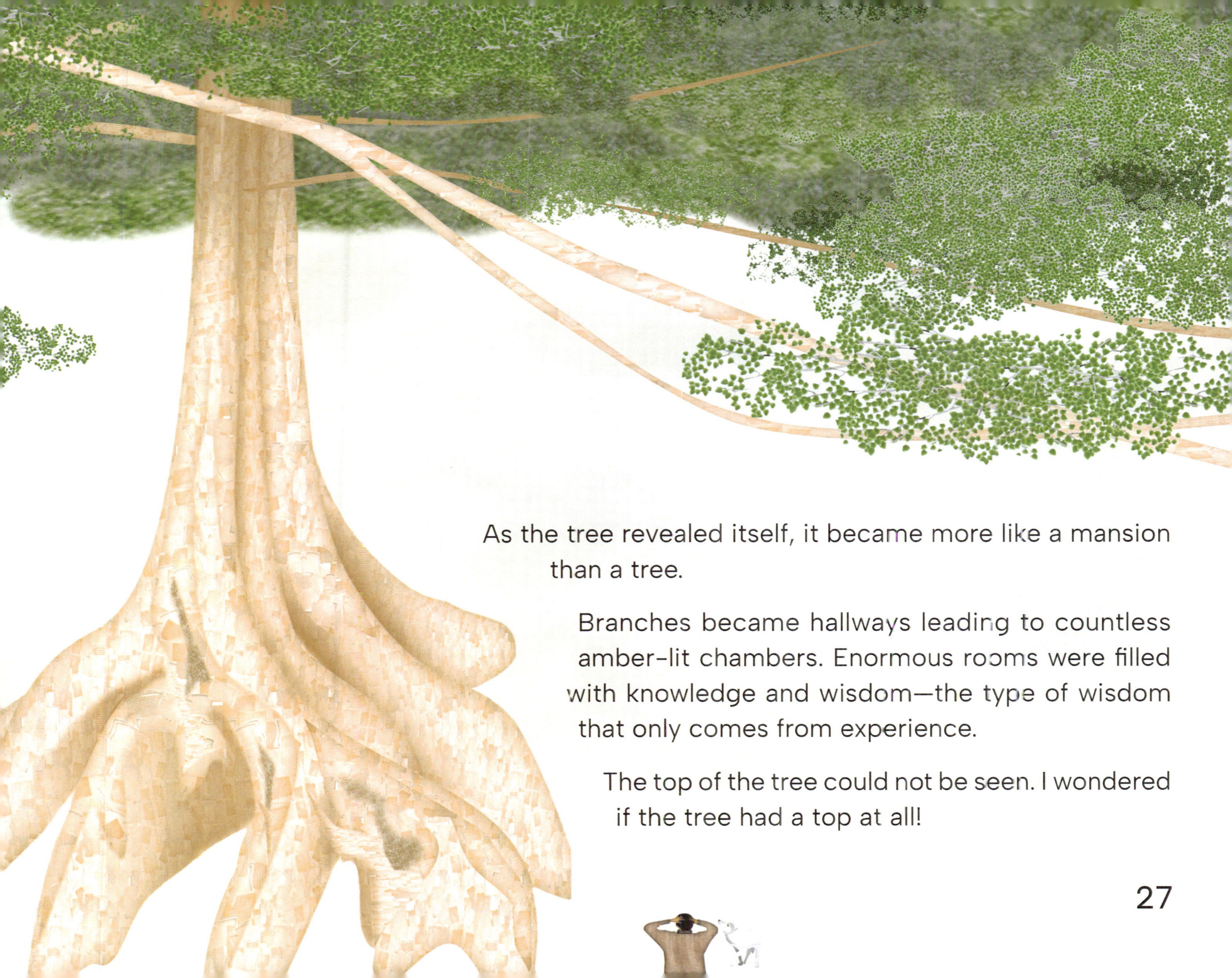

As the tree revealed itself, it became more like a mansion than a tree.

Branches became hallways leading to countless amber-lit chambers. Enormous rooms were filled with knowledge and wisdom—the type of wisdom that only comes from experience.

The top of the tree could not be seen. I wondered if the tree had a top at all!

Back in ordinary reality, I excitedly told Coach of my discovery. She was pleased.

"Does your tree have a name?" she asked.

"No, I didn't catch a name, but I could sense that the tree was a He. He didn't speak to me in actual words, but somehow conveyed to me a sense of great wisdom. I got the feeling of benevolent strength and safety in that wisdom. Really, I wasn't sure what to say or how to say it. I mean, how do you talk to a tree?" I asked.

Coach didn't provide a direct answer. "On your next journey, ask your tree for permission to come inside." she said.

The next day I called White Wolf. He greeted me silently, and we dove into the portal. When we reached the tree, he was just as magnificent as before. He seemed to be waiting for me. Expecting me. Inviting me to enter.

Wolf urged me to jump into the tree. My first leap took me no higher than a few feet onto the base of the tree's gigantic trunk. It was like standing on the toe of a giant.

The tree patiently watched as I looked back to White Wolf for further instruction. Wolf spoke again.

"Don't jump onto the tree, jump into the tree," he said.

Unsure how to do that, I gave it a shot, only to find I had landed on another toe. Wordlessly, Wolf urged me to keep trying. I jumped several more times as White Wolf and the Tree watched intently.

I took a deep breath, felt my desire to merge with the Tree, made one more leap and, this time, it worked!

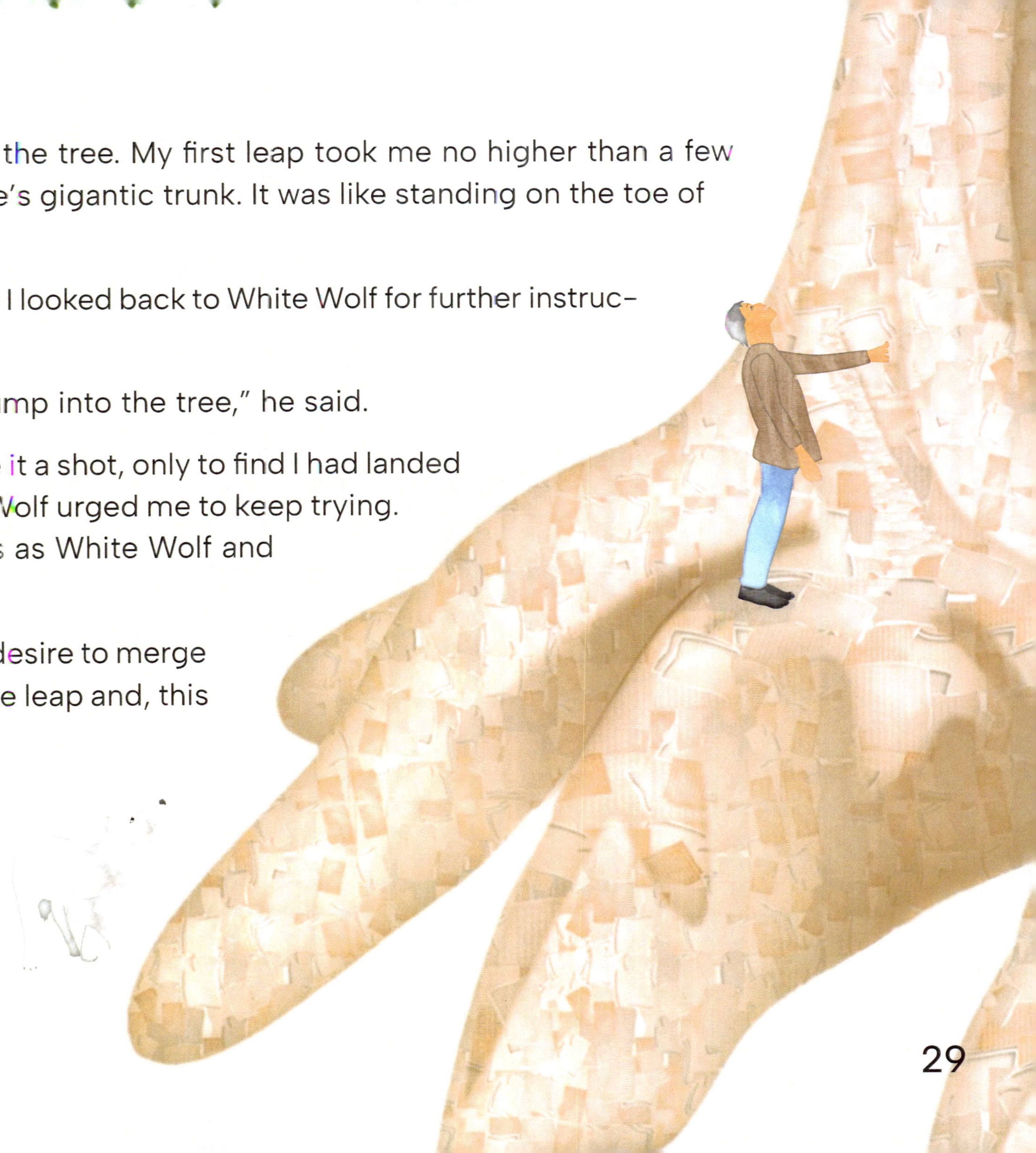

I found myself IN the TREE.

merged!

My muscles became rivers of strength as my body yawned in every direction growing taller and wider with each stretch. I marveled at the strength of my upper body.

My arms reached up far beyond my sight, and I could feel my fingers become delicate, intricate and more flexible the taller I became.

Then my legs plunged deeply down. Massive. Determined. They tunneled down through the nebulous murky ground that was much like the surrounding haze, turning from two to four to eight to sixteen individual leg-roots.

I could see out from every part of the Tree.

Tree shared his amazing strength with me. His knowledge embraced me—his wisdom somehow cocooned me in safety. I felt grounded. Calm. And serene.

Quite different from the man I had come to know as "the burglar"—the man who did not deserve to live a life in his own body.

White Wolf and I often journeyed to rest in Tree's embrace. There, I felt peaceful and calm, cradled in the safety of Tree's strength and wisdom. When I merged with Tree, I became larger than myself. I was uplifted and humbled and loved—all at the same time. My time with Tree was always healing.

Eventually, I decided to build my Garden right next to him. But my first task was to remove that murky haze that still surrounded Tree and obscured my view. This haze was not a cloud nor a wall. It could not be painted on or blown away. Perplexed, I pushed my fingers into it and—to my surprise—an area of haze, a bit larger than my hand, dissolved like fine foam. Behind it was a lovely sky-blue color. I touched the haze in other places and watched it dissolve and the sky-blue color shine through.

The following day, I journeyed back to Tree and asked him for help. We merged, and I felt my fingers become an extension of Tree's top branches. Together, we pushed into the murky darkness and dissolved into wide swaths of haze. The sky-blue color appeared above and around us, giving me a better view to plan my Garden. But I wanted to see farther.

"Can you please take me higher into your top branches so I can better see where I am?"

Tree gently held me, and we grew taller and taller. What happened next left me breathless!

We were so high I saw the curvature of the entire Earth!

It was beautiful, but when I looked down, I got scared. Could I fall? Wanting to return to the ground without revealing my fear, I tried to cajole White Wolf to help me.

"Wouldn't it be fun to ride on your back and float down to the ground?" I asked. He said, "No," sensing my ploy.

Then I heard Tree say wordlessly, "Trust."

"How?" I asked.

"Let go," Tree replied. "Imagine your fear is a feather. Picture it in your hand, then let it slip from your fingers."

A feather appeared in my hand. I held it out in the great void of space before me and let it go.

I watched the feather float harmlessly away. Suddenly, the fear of falling no longer had power over me. In fact, a new strength had replaced that fear.

As I watched the world slowly spin below me, Tree spoke again—not with words, but as if complete patterns of understanding were impressed upon my mind.

"I am your Sacred Tree. I am dedicated to you and hold knowledge that will help you in your life. You can always find me in your Garden, which is a place where you can rest and learn, where you can be healed and restored."

We remained merged in peaceful silence for quite some time. When I returned to the ground, I felt stronger, somehow wiser, and very much loved. I stepped through the portal back into ordinary realm, White Wolf padding by my side.

Back in ordinary reality, Coach listened intently to my recent journeys. (I kept a journal of my journeys, which I emailed for her to review.)

"You say Tree held great knowledge…"

"And great strength and safety," I excitedly interrupted. "I've never thought of safety as being based in knowledge. It is an unusual, all-encompassing safeness. I didn't feel like a small and needy person being sheltered by this enormous talking tree. I felt emotionally sturdy—as if I had the anchoring foundation of large roots and the strength and beauty of Tree's architecture in my torso and arms."

"In your notes, you wrote Tree taught you to trust. In what did he teach you to trust?"

"I guess to trust him."

"Why would he want you to trust him? Does he need your trust?" she asked.

"Well…no. Not like with a parent, or a friend, or God. Tree seems to be self-reliant. He doesn't want or need anything from me," I answered.

"He has great compassion toward me, but he doesn't need reciprocation—although he knows how grateful I am to merge with him. And he accepted that gratitude without conditions."

I listened to myself and paused. I didn't seem to make any sense.

"Well," Coach stepped into the moment of silence, "*how* did Tree teach you to trust?"

"I was at the very top of Tree, above the earth. First, he told me to hold a feather and then to let it go."

"What happened?"

"The feather just floated away."

"And who let the feather go?"

"I did." I looked at Coach for more clues, as I wasn't sure what she was getting at.

"Remember, Frank, that everything that occurs in your Garden represents some aspect in your life," she said. "So, who did you learn to trust when you let the feather go?"

I thought about it, but the answer I found sounded strange coming from my lips.

"Myself?" I offered.

Coach smiled. "If someone hurt you as much as you say you have hurt yourself, would you trust that person?"

I thought about some of the things I blamed myself for. "Of course not." I answered.

"Then how much do you trust yourself?"

"Not very much at all!" I answered, but upon hearing my own words, it felt like a surprisingly jarring betrayal. I broke my eye contact with Coach and stared at my feet, embarrassed.

"So, who is it you need to trust?" Coach asked quietly.

"Myself," I answered.

"This was a good journey. Remember also that every time something changes in your Garden, you may notice a similar change in your ordinary reality. Look for those changes," she said.

I already sensed change.

The realization that I had been betraying myself all these years made me feel sad about how much I had hurt myself—and how often.

I was not feeling self-pity. It was weird, like I was sad for someone else. I didn't quite understand. All I knew was that I did not want to betray myself again—even though I also knew that I likely would.

But at least the next time, I might become aware of what I'm doing.

CHAPTER FOUR

VISITORS

On my next journey, I returned to Tree and discovered a low wooden gate about waist-high nearby. It looked like a gate drawn for a children's book. Simple. I had my gate!

Three white wooden planks curved across the top. A round post held the gate door on either side.

There was no fence or hedge. The gate stood alone and opened as I approached, as if to welcome me.

Beyond the gate was a path of white steppingstones.

The path also looked like a painted illustration—but I could walk on it!

It led me to a grassy, circular clearing. Tall white birch trees bordered the circle. I stepped inside.

I was beginning to get the hang of this! The more I let go of trying to do anything, the more the Garden took on a life of its own.

But Coach had told me I could do garden work. How could I do and not do at the same time?

Sunlight filtered through the white birch branches and leaves, casting a lacework of soft shadows on the ground and across my arms and legs. This spot felt like the perfect place to daydream.

I lay back and dreamed of what I would like in my Garden.

Tree and White Wolf stood by, watching.

First, I thought it might be nice to have a cobblestone floor in part of my Garden. And there it was! Wanting to make it welcoming, I thought of a small round wicker table and two wicker chairs for someone to sit and talk.

Or maybe a visitor would like to walk with me. That made me think of a path around the Garden's cobble-stone floor.

And, voilà!

I gave it a test walk while pondering what to add next.

A fountain? Nah. A birdbath? No.

I seem to be discussing these ideas with some other being and suddenly realized that I was not alone.

I turned to see who it was.

It was my Aunt Lauretta! She had passed away several years ago, and I was overjoyed to see her again. Her presence filled me with love and happiness, just like when I visited her at her home to discuss cats, religion, watercolor paintings, and her tomato plants over tea.

Today she spoke—without words—about mending my broken heart. She was very concerned about all my disappointments. She reached out and placed her hand on my chest. Her warmth soothed my tired heart.

Then Aunt Lauretta let me know that another spirit was eager to greet me, and she left as quietly and softly as she had arrived.

I stood there amazed at how I could reconnect with a person so dear to me, in my Garden, even though she is no longer with us.

Anticipating a chance to entertain other guests in my Garden, I busied myself to make it look even more inviting.

My Aunt Lauretta was Italian, like me, so I decided to continue decorating with a Mediterranean theme, with a bowl of ripe figs, a decanter of red wine, and two glasses on the white wicker table. Nice! Next, a clear glass vase with an arrangement of wildflowers.

That completed, I was drawn to walk down the cobblestone path that circled the Garden and announced, “I am going for a walk and am open for company on my stroll!”

Soon after, I sensed someone was walking with me.

Wow!

I listened for a message but could not make one out. It was just a warm, friendly, feminine presence. I got just what I had asked for.

Company!

I returned to the table, where the wildflowers were so lovely, I thought it would make a nice watercolor.

No sooner did I think that than an easel and brush magically appeared. So, I began to paint.

The feeling of the brush gliding across the canvas brought me a deep, heart-stirring joy.

In that moment, I became aware of the spirit once more and felt like a child, carefree and totally absorbed in what I was doing. The rest of the world disappeared—except for this wonderful new spirit.

She stood beside me, lifted a brush, and started to paint. At first, we painted on separate easels. Then we painted on the same easel.

Then we painted with the
same hand and brush.

Then we painted onto the air itself.

Who was this wonderful spirit?!

Somehow, I knew her very well, and she knew me just as fully.

She lay down the brush and took my hand.

We slowly rose into the air above the wicker table and chairs. Then we flew slowly in long arcs above the cobblestone floor.

It was thrilling!

This spirit was a child. I named her Leila, for a character I had created in a short story when I was twenty.

We instantly became inseparable friends. She seemed to be a childhood kindred spirit, but I could not recall either a person or a place.

Her smiles warmed my heart. Leila was playfully impulsive and innocent, wanting only to be my friend and to have fun. She was utterly free, her mind unencumbered by expectations. She had no fear. No hesitation.

As we moved gracefully through the air, I felt as carefree as a child. New, and yet complete. Uncomplicated. My heart was a happy toddler, no longer heavy with years of loneliness and disappointment.

And then something healed in my heart, and I learned something about myself. Or maybe I knew it all along but forgot. And here it is:

Although my life had been heavy and held to the ground, my true nature was to fly.

CHAPTER FIVE

THE DIFFERENT SPIRITS

I began to anticipate my visits with Leila in my Garden. Sometimes we would sit on soft mats and levitate above the cobblestone floor, surrounded in silence, feeling wonderfully whole in each other's presence. At other times, we would dance and twirl around the Garden and the cobblestone floor in mid-air.

Leila's presence became a constant. Her sunny nature warmed everything, and she was always ready to smile and have fun with me during my

journeys. When I became aware of her presence in my mind and heart in ordinary reality, I reached out to Coach to ask who she was.

"I feel Leila's happiness while weeding, uncovering earthworms, and placing them safely back into fresh soil. This is taking place in my backyard, not in the Garden of my journeys!" I said.

"I sense her delight in simple beauty. In tiny flowers. While listening to music. When I draw, or feel the thrill of an approaching thunderstorm. The intensity of her joy makes my heart float in my chest and energizes my entire body!"

"You said she seems to be a childhood friend?" Coach asked.

"Yes. But I can't remember who. Cousins, neighborhood kids. No one comes to mind. But I know her completely!"

"How would you describe your relationship to Leila?" Coach asked.

"Well, we really don't talk much, but it's clear that Leila wants to be with me in daily life—not because she loves me—but because she loves life. She is aware of my trauma and sorrows, and still wants to enjoy life through me, regardless of that pain. And when I share those moments of intense joy with her, I feel safe, happy and complete."

"You know Leila well, because she is a part of you," Coach said. I tried to understand as she continued to explain.

"When we suffer trauma, neglect or abuse, our soul can become fragmented, and parts can be lost or stuck in time. Leila is one such aspect of your soul that you had deliberately and unconsciously suppressed.

"She became lost to you.

"The process of recovering lost souls, or fragments of soul, is called soul retrieval. Leila appears in your Garden now because you have made it a safe place for her to return home to you. Because you did such careful work in your Garden, Leila's appearance there is an example of a spontaneous soul retrieval."

"But Leila seems so real. How is she different from Tree and White Wolf?" I asked. "They seem real to me, too."

"All three are very real, but also uniquely different," Coach replied.

"Sacred Tree and Wolf are powerful, benevolent nature spirits. We call these Spirit Helpers. As such, they are indeed separate from you.

"The more you journey, the more you discover that there is an autonomy in the spirit world. In other words, we are not in control of what the spirits do when we journey. They have a life of their own, which is why we are often surprised and amazed by what occurs. They also have their own distinguishing characteristics and qualities, but remember the job of a Spirit Helper is always to give you power, protection, and support.

"Often these Spirit Helpers have been with us throughout our lifetime, or through many lifetimes. That's why so

many of these Spirit Helpers seem familiar to us—we may even remember them as childhood friends who have been forgotten as we grew older.

"There is a protocol in the spirit world, however, that these helpers will not interfere in our lives until we reach out to connect with them. But when we cross the bridge into non-ordinary reality—as you did when you journeyed to your Sacred Garden—we often find them waiting for us in response to our intention," Coach said.

I listened intently, happy to hear some explanation of the inexplicable. My journey encounters had been so unexpectedly vivid, compelling, and invoked so many different emotions and thoughts, that I was longing for a framework in which to understand them.

"What about my Aunt Lauretta?" I asked. "I did not invite her to visit—though I am very glad she did."

"Aunt Lauretta is an Ancestral Spirit. Your Sacred Garden is a wonderful place to meet with your ancestors, especially those who are willing to come forward with unconditional love and support. Remember the beautiful wicker table and chairs you placed there? You instinctively wanted a place for visitors, and Aunt Lauretta appeared in response to your own intention to find companionship and comfort."

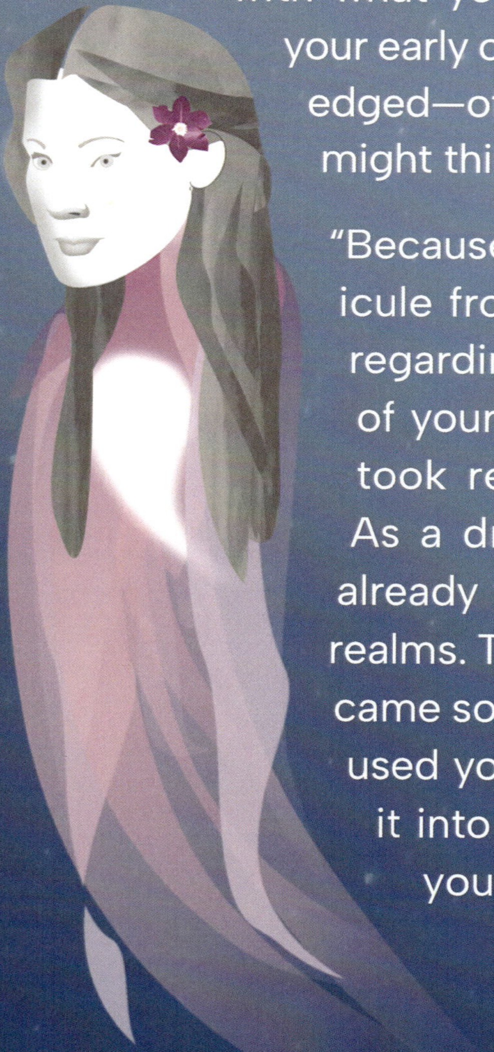

"So, Tree, White Wolf and my Aunt Lauretta exist on their own as independent spirits, while Leila is part of my own soul." I asked. "Did I get that right?"

"Yes. From the way you described Leila, along with what you have shared with me about your early childhood, she is the unacknowledged—often bullied—part of yourself you might think of as your Magical Child.

"Because you experienced so much ridicule from your family at an early age regarding the artistic, feminine aspect of your personality, Leila split off and took refuge in non-ordinary reality. As a dreamy young child, you were already very familiar with these liminal realms. That's why creating your Garden came so naturally to you. And when you used your creative imagination to turn it into a warm and welcoming place, you discovered Leila was already there waiting for you," Coach explained.

Her words brought tears to my eyes, which I quickly wiped away. It was so very beautiful—a stark contrast to the self-hatred I learned when I was a child and carried with me throughout my life.

"What you experienced was a spontaneous retrieval of this soul part who was ready to come home. The work ahead of you," Coach continued, "is the work of integrating this part into your present personality.

"Spend time with her in your Garden, ask her what she needs to receive from you in order to feel safe and welcome, and invite her into your heart where she can become part of your ordinary reality."

"But I enjoy my time with Leila in my Sacred Garden so much," I said, worried. "If she enters my heart and agrees to return with me to ordinary reality, will I still be able to fly with her in my Garden?"

"Any time you want!" Coach answered.

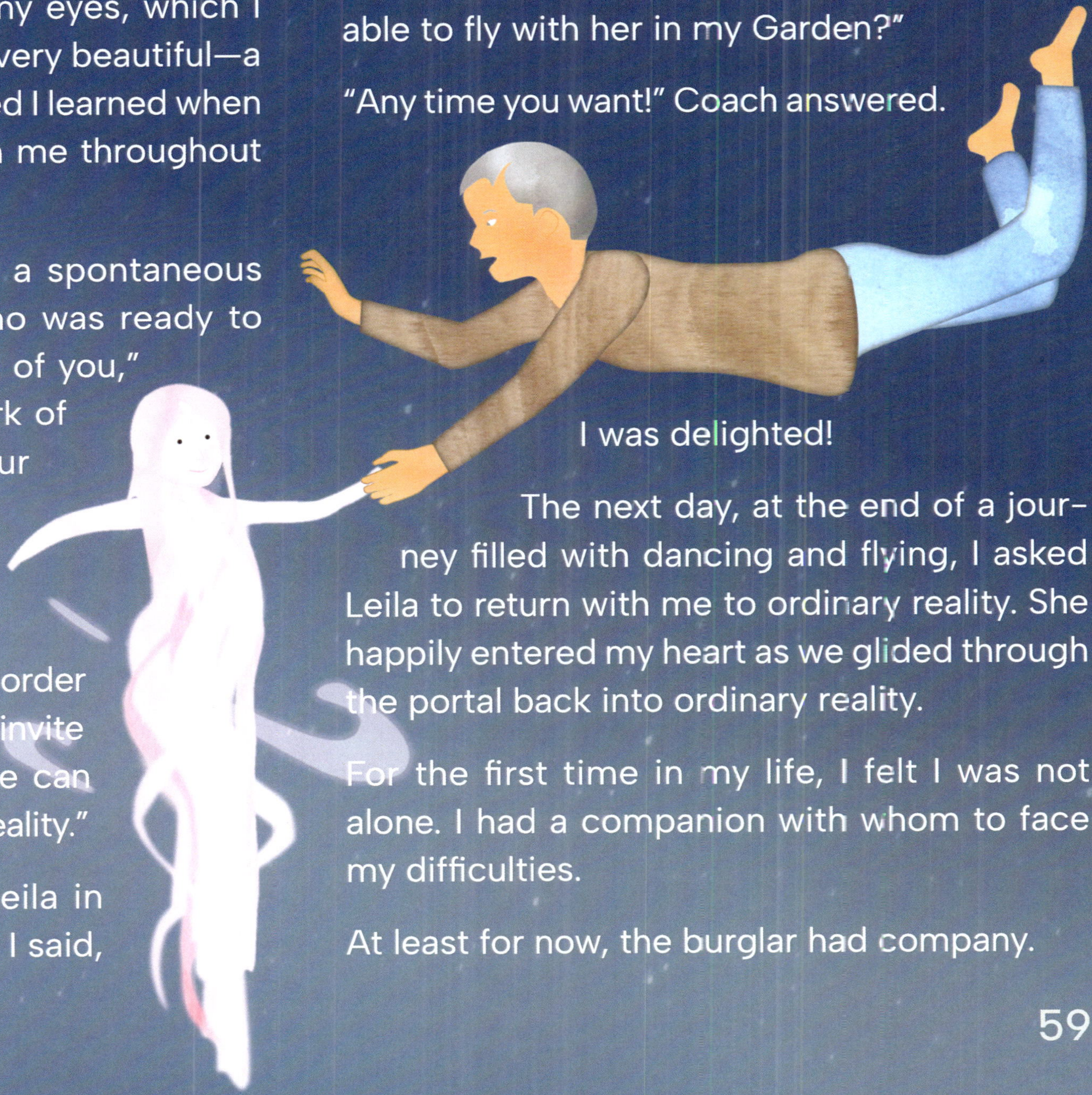

I was delighted!

The next day, at the end of a journey filled with dancing and flying, I asked Leila to return with me to ordinary reality. She happily entered my heart as we glided through the portal back into ordinary reality.

For the first time in my life, I felt I was not alone. I had a companion with whom to face my difficulties.

At least for now, the burglar had company.

CHAPTER SIX
TEACHER

Coach continued to help me expand and explore my Sacred Garden.

"Make the Garden your own," she would remind me. "This is your Sacred Garden. It belongs to no one else." So, during one of my journeys to the Garden, I stopped at the gate and gave it some thought. Maybe a sign on the gate would better signify this Garden was uniquely and utterly mine.

First, I wrote "Frank's Garden" across the wooden planks, but that didn't resonate with me at all. I just didn't like seeing my name there. Even though I was making progress, I still considered my name to be synonymous with failure.

I decided not to use a name at all. Instead, I painted a simple cheery image of a smiling cat's face.

That felt perfect!

To my delight, the drawing continued to smile from the gate's white planks on subsequent journeys.

Truth is, visits to my Garden were becoming more and more frequent, and the Garden itself was becoming more defined and consistent. Sacred Tree was always there near the gate. The wicker furniture, cobblestone floor, the birch trees and meditation pillows were always at the ready.

What was changing was me.

Meanwhile, life in ordinary reality was also improving. I was pleased to find myself more emotionally resilient and enjoying moments of life more fully. Coach was providing me with insightful and helpful techniques to become centered, grounded, and empowered. With her help, I was assembling a "tool kit" of practices that strengthened my ability to manage my emotions and thoughts in ordinary reality.

But this was just a start. These improvements helped me begin to see that there was still more work to be done.

Often, sometimes hourly, I struggled with the strange anxiety of not belonging in my body, nor in my life. Entrenched thoughts of self-loathing and doubt would tug at my feet, trying to drag me back to despair. Coach urged me to bring this pain to the Garden and ask for help. This was not an easy thing to do.

I was scared to find out just how deep my hurt ran. I knew from my therapy experiences that emotional healing can be messy, painful stuff.

Coach, however, reassured me about the power and efficacy of working with my spirit helpers in non-ordinary reality for both physical and emotional healing.

"Healing an emotional wound is similar to healing a physical wound in that both must be uncovered, brought into the light, cleansed, and healed," she said. Meanwhile, in non-ordinary reality, White Wolf reminded me that courage cannot exist without the presence of fear. I took that to heart and thanked him.

Eventually the day came when I felt ready to bring my big hurts to the Garden. I bundled them together—the sadness and disappointment that my life, at 60, was not filled with the memories of love, friendship, and accomplishments I've watched other people attain in their lives. I topped off the bundle with the disturbing details from the childhood trauma vividly revealed in my early journey that had ended up in a smoldering firepit.

With White Wolf bounding by my side, giving me power, protection, and support, we glided through the portal.

Once through, I opened the gate, slowly approached my Garden and looked around.

And there, waiting patiently...

...was a new spirit.

She seemed distinctly different from the other spirits I had met, yet her very countenance drew me closer. She glowed with friendship and her gaze revealed a complete acceptance of me as she smiled warmly.

This spirit seemed familiar, and I sensed she knew me far better than I knew myself. But I did not know who she was at all. Was she an ancestor I had never gotten to know?

She gently touched my face. I looked into her eyes and felt complete trust.

Then she spoke.

"I am your guide and your advocate. When you become world-weary, find me and look into my eyes. I am here to give you sanctuary and to assist you in life. I know what you know. I feel what you feel. I know what you need. I have many things to share that will help you get through your days," she said.

She then stopped talking and simply gazed at me, happy to have my attention. There was no hurry to reveal anything more at that time, so we meditated together, floating several feet above the cobblestone Garden floor. Then we simply sat. We smiled. Just being in her presence was calming and restorative.

I wanted to call her by name, but nothing fit. So, because she said she would teach me, I decided to call her Teacher.

Soon after that first meeting, I sensed Teacher in ordinary reality too—always with kindness and support and always as my advocate. Sometimes she would simply observe me. When she offered insight, it was always pertinent and given in a manner that helped me learn and grow.

She and I interacted in ways that were very different from Tree and Wolf.

For one thing, we talked more frequently and more directly to each other. We spoke without words, discerning each other's thoughts and feelings quicker than words could ever form.

Coach clarified this wonderful spirit's role.

"You aptly named her Teacher, as she is coming to you as a Spirit Teacher. This type of spirit is distinct from the Spirit Helpers who come from the realm of Nature—such as White Wolf, your Sacred Tree, and the kittens who appeared to show you the way to your Garden. As we've said, the job of these Spirit Helpers is to give you power, protection and support.

"Spirit Teachers, on the other hand, inhabit the realm of ascended masters, great spiritual teachers, healers or scholars from the past, angels or deities. They often appear in human form to help us further our knowledge of ourselves."

I listened, feeling awed yet shyly undeserving. "But why me, and why now?" I asked.

"Frank, your efforts to find healing are significant, sincere, and without malice. Those efforts have not gone unnoticed. Remember the old saying? When the student is ready, the Teacher will appear?" she said. "You are ready, Frank, so your Teacher has appeared."

CHAPTER SEVEN

TWO BODIES

One day while meditating with Teacher in the Garden—I've been a meditator most of my adult life and I thought, why not meditate in my Garden?—my mind drifted from my usual mantra. Knowing my self-critical nature and impatience with myself, Teacher quietly encouraged me to return to the mantra.

I did and continued meditating a while longer when my mind drifted again. I became angry with myself. Teacher stopped meditating and looked at me with great patience and understanding.

"Here, please let me show you something that will help," she said. I did not know what she had in mind and simply listened.

"Your body," she began, "is an amazing vessel for your spirit to reside in. It does not simply contain your spirit the way a glass vase holds a bouquet. A vase cannot remember every flower it has held, nor can it recall the flower's beauty and eventual decay.

"Your body, in contrast, records all the joys and sorrows, hurts and triumphs of life. These memories reside in your cells—in your body's sinews, bones and organs.

"Unfortunately, this can make the human body a complicated and crowded place. Memories of emotional, psychological, and physical pain can stress vital organs. Trauma becomes stored in tissues that are prone to disease.

"Negative body memory is often evidenced by a person's attitudes, actions and, of course, the maladies they suffer from.

"Fortunately, the spirit body is spacious and mercifully unaffected by the classic laws of physics, such as gravity and entropy.

"While our physical body is defined by space and finite in time, our spirit body is limitless and infinite."

I listened in awe.

"Your spirit body has much more power than your physical body," she continued. "The self-hatred that afflicts your physical body has no power in your spirit body. In fact, your spirit body can help reduce that negative influence in your life.

"Let me show you," she smiled. "First, take a look inside your physical body."

I have no idea how, but I found myself looking inside my body and saw that it was inundated by clutter—my own hurtful clutter!

Anger lay poised like taut tripwires, ready to slice through delicate vital organs.

Hopelessness, fear, and frustration twisted my guts into knots.

Noise filled my head. Insults echoed from all directions. Hundreds of old files chronicled my every dashed hope.

Reams of abandoned life plans painfully pressed upon the back of my eyeballs and slipped through cracks and crevices in my skull.

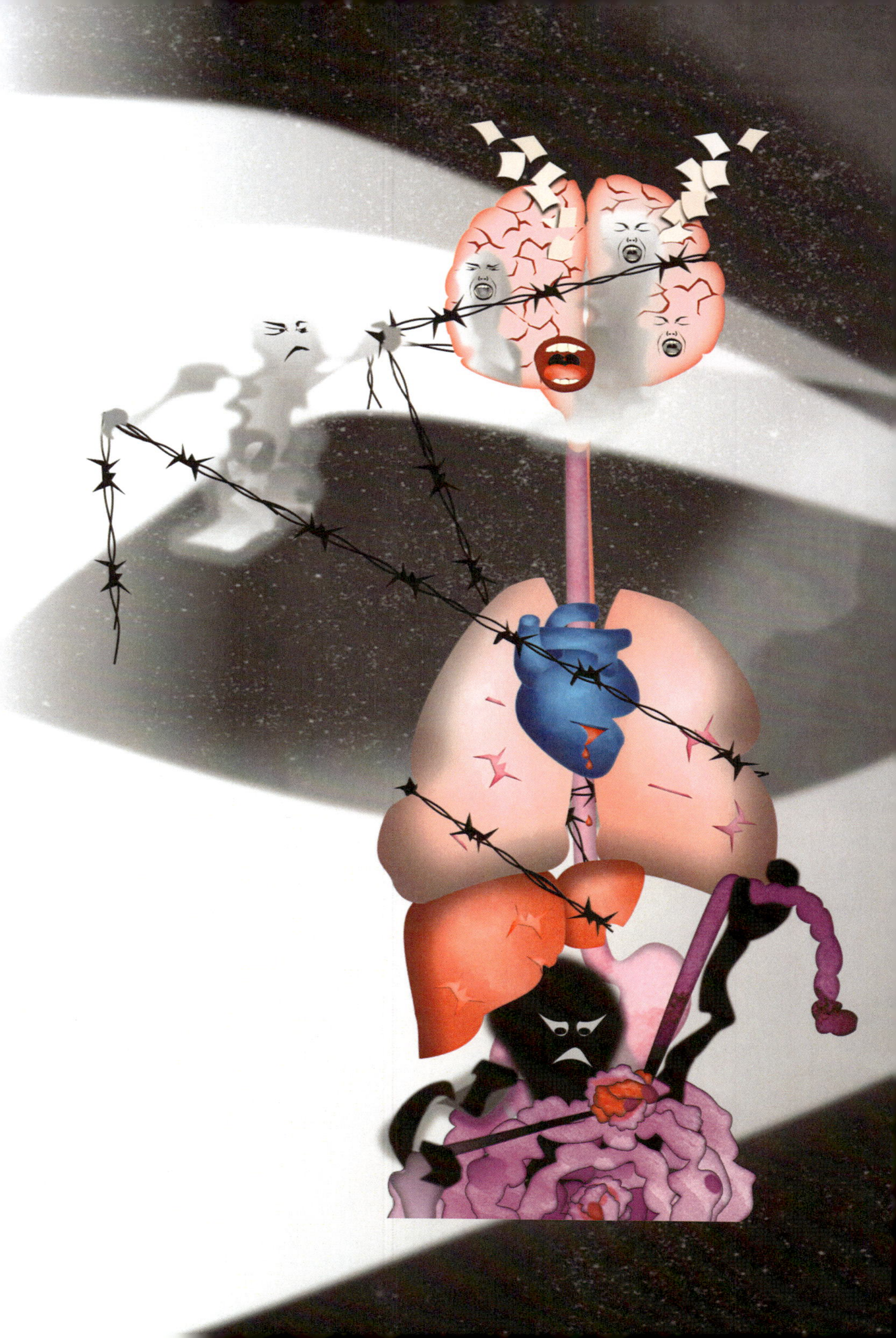

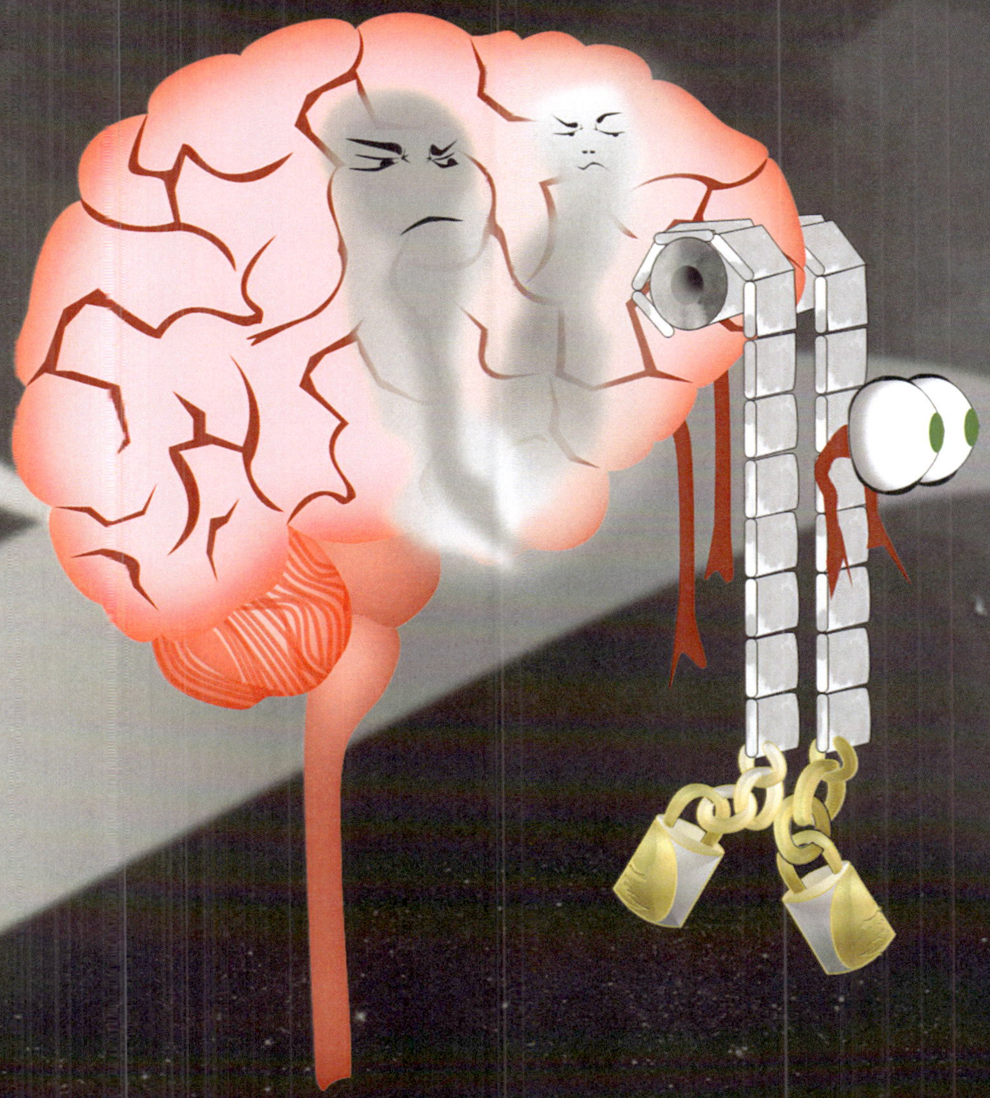

And, yes, blocking my eyes like padlocked steel shutters was my self-hatred, keeping me from seeing anything but my own failing.

My body was being held hostage by my emotions, toxic thoughts, and memories of a life I felt I had ruined with constant failure.

"Now, take a look at your spirit body," Teacher continued.

To my amazement, suddenly I was no longer inside of my physical body, and I could see all around me, the night sky stretching in all directions.

I seemed to be in a vast field, and then ***I was*** the field.

Inside me was clarity and calm. Order and peace.

"Now look again from your physical body, and compare it with your spirit body," Teacher urged. I did.

First, from the physical body, then from the spirit body. Physical. Spirit. Physical. Spirit.

Again, and again.

I saw how different they were! I felt empowered, even hopeful.

Teacher continued speaking.

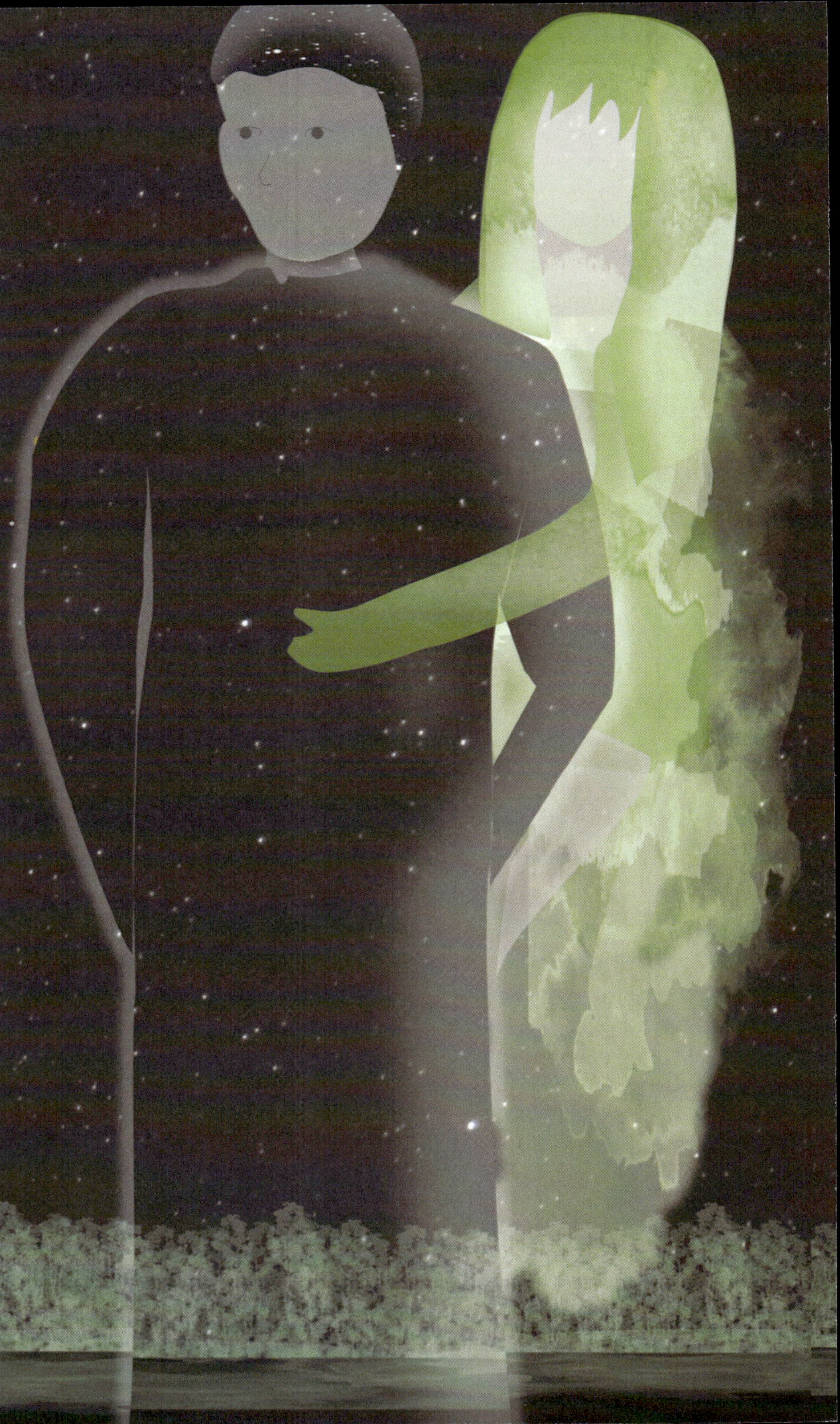

"Life is perceived very differently when a person lives mostly or completely from the physical body. It can be very difficult and painful to get through life.

"Flesh and bone do to people what blinders do to horses: it greatly narrows their field of vision. Seeing and living from your spirit body, even just now and then, will always help you in life. But that is not always easy."

"Our perception of life is often dominated by the physical body. It grabs and holds our attention with its immediacy and insistence. Its pleasures are irresistible. Its threats of pain are terrifying. The actual pain can be torturous.

"Just try to remember that the physical world is not your only reality."

And with that, the lesson ended. Teacher smiled softly in a way that said she trusted me with the knowledge she had shared.

Her trust was well placed. In the weeks to come, I found myself remembering my visions and gradually growing in self-confidence. I noticed moments, then entire days, where I was less critical of myself.

That knowledge, along with the support and guidance I was getting from Coach, was preparing me to bring my deepest pain to the Garden.

When I finally did, I had an unexpected and profound encounter.

CHAPTER EIGHT

WHERE'S THE PAIN?

The following week proved to be especially challenging. There were so many encounters to trigger my self-doubt that I found myself spiraling into depression. I sought Coach's counsel.

"I've been more aware of the voices in my head telling me I am a failed man who is unworthy of happiness ever since Teacher showed me my two bodies, the spiritual body and the physical," I said.

"That is not uncommon," Coach said. "Recognizing a problem often makes its occurrence more apparent. You are on the right path.

Emotional wellness and healing are not like flipping a switch. Rather, it's a process. Or you might think of it as the unraveling of processes you've been implementing as survival strateg es throughout your lifetime."

"But I still feel like I don't belong in this world," I said. "It's a feeling I have had all my adult life. Somehow, I am not the sum of my parts, and it makes me want to simply disappear from the world," I tried to explain.

"That's a very cogent description of your pain. Now tell me, where do you feel this pain?" Coach asked.

The question didn't make sense to me.

"My mind. I guess. I can't find my missing parts—as if I was born incomplete," I said.

"That sounds painful. Can you describe what that pain feels like in your body?" she said.

"Well, there is confusion in my brain. Lots of noisy, conflicting thoughts. You see, it all started with a situation yesterday when..."

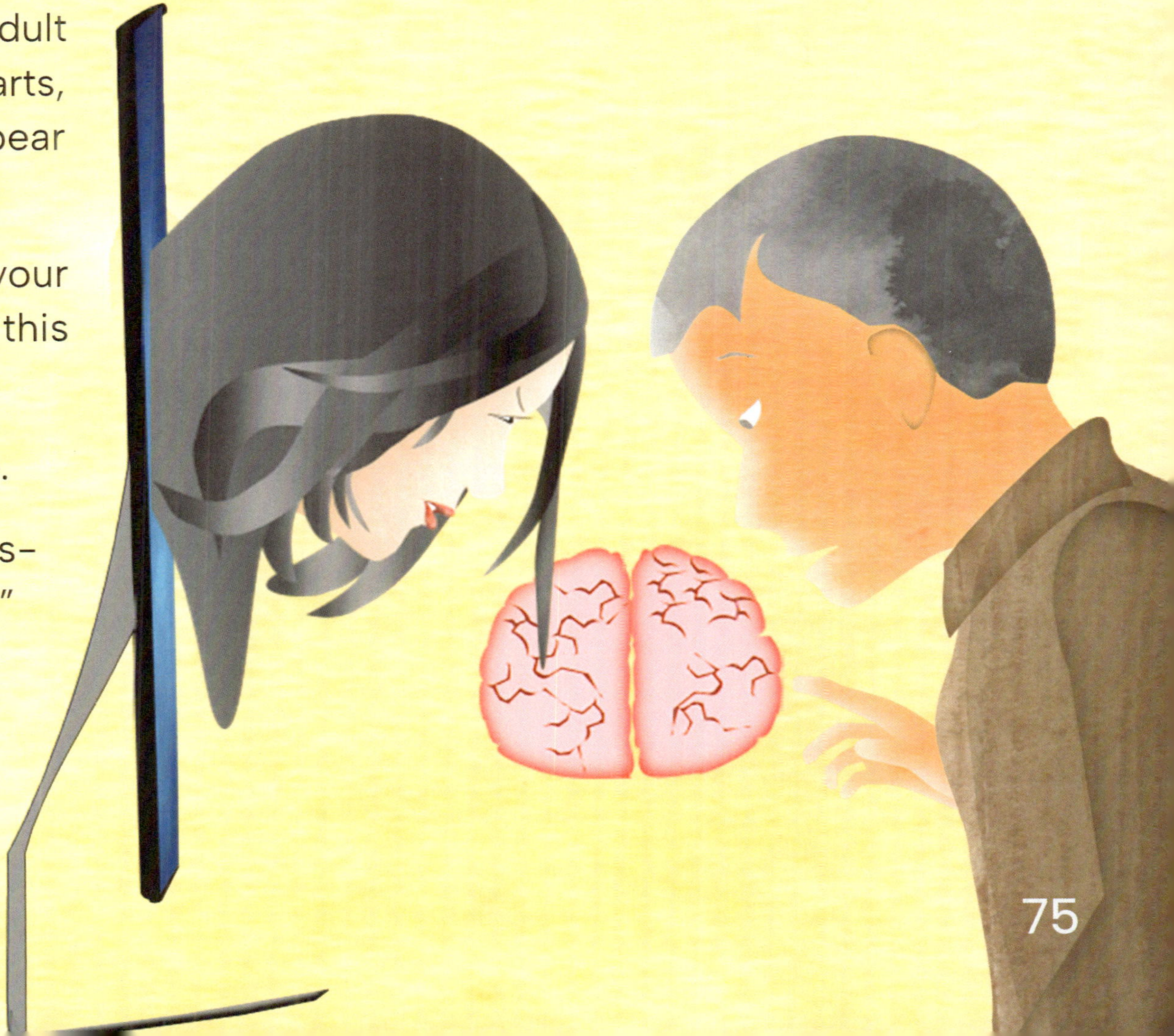

Over the decades, counselors would ask me to talk about my thoughts, issues, conflicts and the minutia of my conversations and encounters. The process made me think of panning for that one gold nugget that would make the days, months, and years spent in therapy worth it. Then everything would fall into place for me.

This, of course, never happened.

Coach understood her approach was new for me, and helped me find what I thought was kind of nuts; a physical, bodily pain corresponding to my emotional pain.

"Breathe deeply. Relax. Take your time," she demonstrated. Then together we took long, slow, deep breaths. I relaxed into my breath.

"No," Coach cut me off decisively, holding up her hand. I stopped talking.

"It won't help you go into your story—or to think your way around your emotions. You already know what the feelings are," she said. "Just tell me: ***where in your body*** do you experience the emotion?"

Emotion in my body?! This was a novel idea.

"Now," Coach asked again, "try to sense where the pain is located in your body."

I remained silent for a few minutes.

Listening... Breathing...

And then, suddenly, there it was.

"It's my heart! I feel a pain in my heart! IT'S IN MY HEART!" I exclaimed, proud to make this new discovery.

"I feel it. I feel it," I rushed on, "but I don't know why it's there. I don't know how to soothe it. Or what to do with it. Maybe it's from..."

Coach put up her hand again.

"Don't try to explain the pain. Simply acknowledge it, and try to feel it," she said.

"How can I acknowledge something if I don't even know what it is?" I complained.

"Okay," Coach continued patiently. "Try saying these words: my heart hurts."

"My heart hurts," I mouthed flatly.

"Hmm, that doesn't sound like pain to me," Coach responded.

So, I dropped the sarcasm, took a breath and tried to be honest enough with myself to feel the pain—just for a brief moment—before repeating those words. But I was so shocked to feel the depth of that pain that I was afraid to even try.

Coach could see the panic creeping into my eyes.

"Frank, if you are hurt and have pain, you are entitled to say that you are in pain. If you need to cry it, then cry it. If you need to scream it, then do so."

Now, I had long felt that crying was a selfish act. I never allowed it for myself. I had never cried in front of other counselors, and I didn't want to start now. Coach sensed this and provided space for me.

"Many of us try to think away our pain. We think if we can understand it with our minds, it will go away. This is natural. Pain is, after all, painful. It's human nature to create all sorts of strategies to prevent us from feeling pain. So, how's that been working for you?"

I swallowed.

"Frank, now that you've uncovered the pain in your heart, your job is to feel it. The only way past it is through it. So don't ignore it, don't explain it away, or try to cover it up. This is an opportunity to express the pain that was too overwhelming for you in the past.

"You don't need to do it with me. You can take this pain into your Sacred Garden and ask Teacher for help. She'll know what to do."

CHAPTER NINE

FINDING FRANKIE

The rest of that week, the pain in my heart grew. None of the cognitive skills I had learned in over twenty years of therapy lessened it, nor did a lifetime of countless rationalizations.

It seemed to take on a life of its own.

Maybe Coach was right.

Finally, with the hurt clearly pounding in my chest, I journeyed to my Garden to find Teacher.

She was expecting me and took my hand.

We sat on the cobblestone floor and Teacher placed one hand on my heart, much as Aunt Lauretta had done, and wrapped her other arm around my shoulders.

I looked into Teacher's eyes.

"I hurt," I told her in a near whisper.

"I hurt!" I said louder. "I am hurt! I am hurt!" I shouted those words like a call for help.

"I am hurt! I am hurt!"

Teacher held me close as the pain in my heart continued to rise and become sharper and more forceful. The pain swelled until it seemed like my heart would burst.

Then it did.

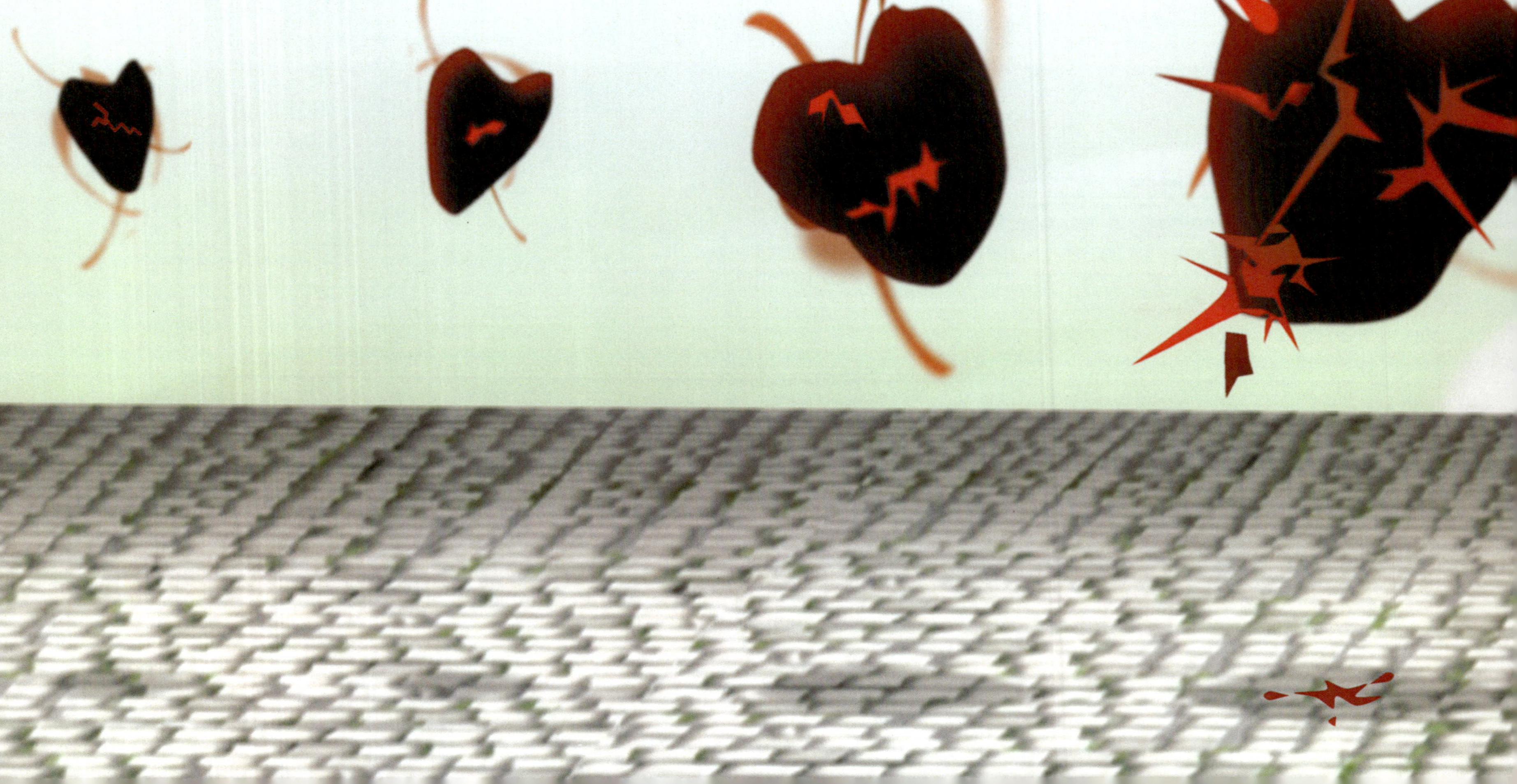

A large, jagged gash ripped across my heart. Blood, sadness, and pain poured out from the wound into my hands. Teacher saw the gash and felt the pain, too.

"I am hurt!" I screamed. Hot tears ran down my face.

We held each other tightly and yelled out loud in unison, "I HURT!" Each time we screamed in pain, Teacher held me closer and closer. My body spasmed as hurt poured from my torn heart.

We cried until exhaustion made way for breathy sobs. Each sob peeled away years of pain, shame, and anguish. I watched as layer after layer peeled away.

It seemed to have no end...

Then, to my astonishment, a last layer of pain peeled away
and uncovered a young man.

He sat sullen on the Garden floor. Head bent, his back to us. But he was aware of our presence.

In him was a dark sadness. I wanted to help him. Yet, he frightened me. His darkness was dangerous.

Volatile.

He didn't want to be seen, but I recognized him. He was me as a young man.

Let's call him Frankie.

Forty years ago, Frankie's world came to a complete stop while everyone else's world continued to spin. Peers finished college, found love, built careers, got married and pursued adventures.

Frankie's sole desire—his career, love and dream—was to make music.

But that dream arrived stillborn.

His repeated attempts to resuscitate the dream failed. Lacking any alternative plan or helping hands, he became trapped inside his parent's house, confined to his room, forced to live beside the decaying corpse of his dream. That room became his prison.

He felt exiled from life.

Only after seeing him, did I realized he was still imprisoned forty years later.

And still tormented.

I had tried so hard to build a life far from him and his dream—but there he remained, trapped inside that room. He was such a tragic, lonely figure!

Teacher and I agreed Frankie needed to be rescued from that dismal room, but how? And why? What would his freedom gain him after forty years in prison?

And could freeing Frankie help me? Was it his continued imprisonment that made me feel like a burglar in my own body?

Frankie never turned around to acknowledge us.
We left him, broken, on the Garden floor.

I needed Coach's guidance
for the next Garden visit.

Back in ordinary reality, I briefed Coach on my encounter and asked for guidance.

"Nice work, Frank. How are you feeling about finding Frankie?" she asked.

I gave it some thought. "Seeing Frankie reminded me of how miserable I was forty years ago," I said. "When Frankie wasn't totally paralyzed, he would kind of deconstruct himself and try to reassemble the pieces in a way that would fit together to create a whole person. But it never worked."

I remembered Frankie would sometimes fantasize that his efforts to be whole finally worked. Lost in reverie, he imagined starting his music career, developing friendships, finding love and restoring his dignity for all his family and lost friends to see. But that day never came.

Then it struck me.

"A WHOLE PERSON...that's all Frankie ever wanted. He just wanted to be a whole person. Whole, just like everybody else." I began to cry.

I realized then that I had been trying to erase any trace of Frankie from my life. I was angry at him for wanting something wonderful, like music, and then blamed him for losing the dream.

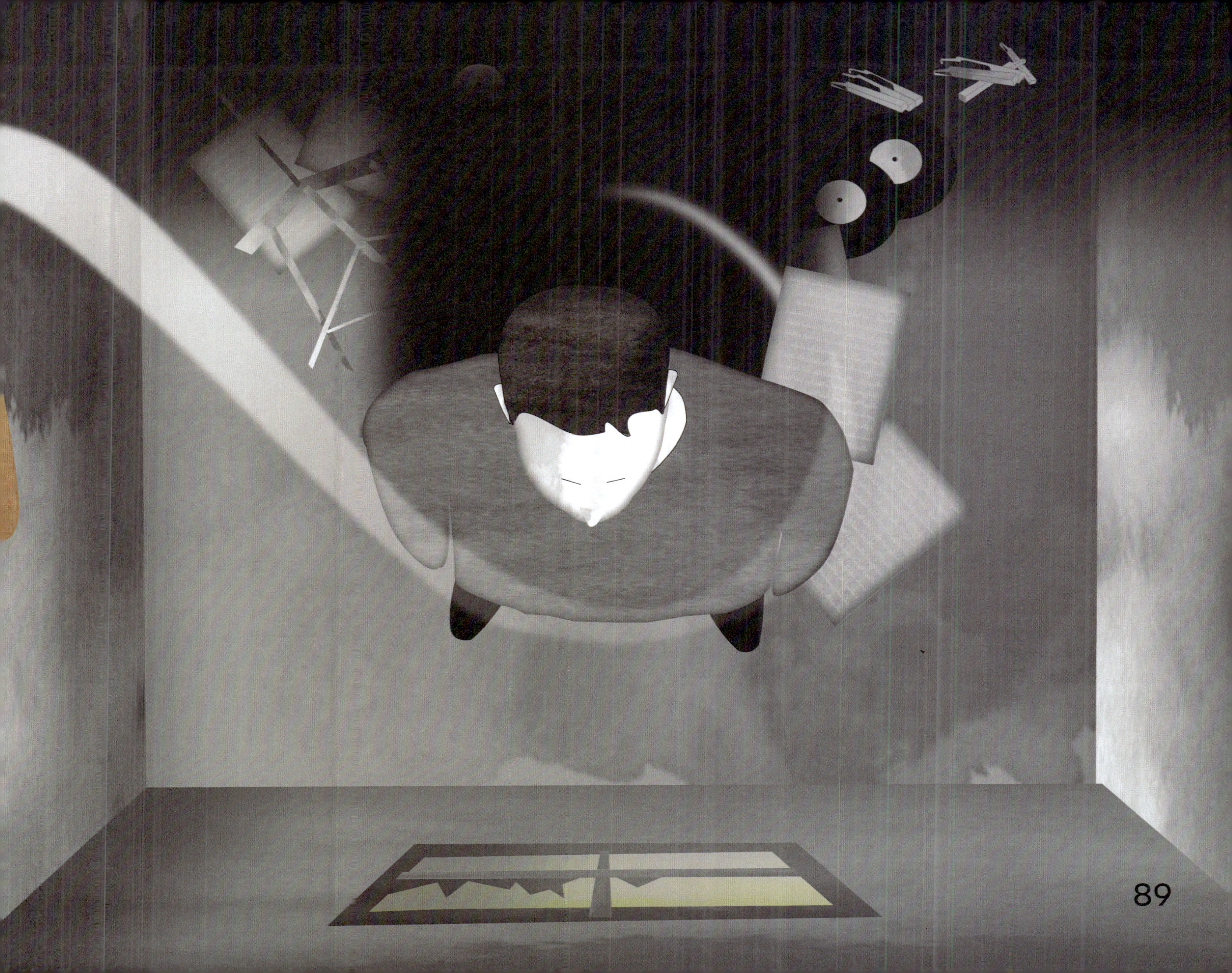

The truth was—more than even music—what Frankie really wanted was what I had longed for my entire life. He and I simply wanted to feel like a whole person.

For the first time in my life, I felt for that young man trapped in his room—his youth wasted like water emptied onto desert sand. Seeing him like this and recognizing his pain led me to feel genuine compassion for him for the very first time.

That's when I realized something important.

"Frankie can never forgive himself," I wept. "Only I can do that."

Coach let me cry and connect with my emotions. She asked quietly, "Can you see any connection between 20-year-old Frankie and your 60-year-old self?"

"Yes. Now I do."

"So, tell me, who is Frankie?" Coach asked?

"He is the creative part of myself I abandoned."

"Yes, and he is more than that. You abandoned your twenty-year-old self and his dreams of creativity. Frankie is that part of your soul that became fragmented when the pain became intolerable. Well done!"

"Huh?!!!" I exclaimed, flabbergasted.

Coach explained, "Now that you've finally found Frankie, your job is to retrieve him from his prison and make sure he has what he needs to thrive. On your next visit to the Garden, call on your spiritual allies, and ask them to help you create a safe place for Frankie in your Garden, where he can start his healing."

I was both astounded and exhausted. "Sounds like a plan," I said.

CHAPTER TEN

THE PLAN

On my next visit, I stood by the Garden gate and called to my Spirit Helpers. Out they came—Teacher, Leila, and White Wolf. They understood the size of the task ahead.

When we entered the Garden, we found Frankie still slumped on the cobblestone floor. I stepped closer and gently, slowly, called his name several times.

He grudgingly turned slightly, eyes clouded. I could feel the bitterness in him. I wanted to comfort him.

"I love you, Frankie," I said awkwardly. My words clanged empty in my ears and an embarrassing, shameful, sheep-ish, shitty feeling suddenly grabbed me.

I was trying to save Frankie, but I'm not a savior. Far from it. I'm a fake.

"Frankie, you...you are whole. You are a whole person," I said, my words trailing into a whisper. Fear tightened my gut and held my breath hostage.

"You no...no longer...you don't need to...to tear yourself apart."

My breathy words of false cheer stumbled from my mouth and transformed into horrible, mean lies. Vile, cynical offers of hope to someone who was beyond hope. I didn't understand why it sounded that way.

My regret surged. My fear grew. Guilt consumed my courage.

I was a murderer returning to the scene of the crime—only to find my victim somehow alive and livid with rage. I was his killer

No reconciliation.
No forgiveness.
None was deserved.

Frankie pulsed with rage. His naked anger scared me. I needed to get hold of myself and remember why I had come in the first place. What was I supposed to say? All that came to mind was that I wanted to show that I was on his side. But my words came out patronizing and pathetic.

"...you can have a happy life here..."
"...look at the trees..."
"...so much beauty..."

Gesturing lamely around the Garden, I realized there was no object, scent or color that might interest him. I watched Frankie's darkness writhe and smolder in my beautiful Garden I had crafted so carefully and enjoyed so thoroughly.

"You and I can make anything you want, Frankie! Would you like a room for yourself in the Garden?"

Frankie turned suddenly and said, "I have a room."

He then set his eyes on me for the first time and repeated in a terrifying low growl,

"I have a room!"

"I have a room!"

I slunk away, desperate to reach the Garden gate.

"WHY DID I OFFER HIM A ROOM?" I cried out to Teacher as I fled.
"All this time I...I thought he was dead...
...but he's alive...trapped in that room...
...all alone...for FORTY YEARS!"

And the journey was over.

CHAPTER ELEVEN

FREEING FRANKIE

Back in ordinary reality, I met with Coach, desperate for advice. "What am I doing wrong, besides everything?" I asked.

"Frankie is hurting," she said. "Don't try to fix his hurt. Instead, try asking him what he needs and how you can help."

Hmmm...

So the next day, I entered the Garden with Teacher, White Wolf and Leila, and set off to find Frankie.

Sure enough, we found him, slouched and sullen, locked in his own black mood.

"What do you need, Frankie? How can I help?" I asked.

He stood slowly and gradually turned his head toward me.

I panicked in the resulting silence and heard myself blurt out, "You can make music!"

He spun around and looked at me in disgust.

I watched in terror as his anger swelled.

Suddenly, I heard Coach's voice in my head reminding me,

"Don't try to fix his hurt. You need to feel his hurt."

I grabbed Frankie and held onto him, tight, feeling his torment, remembering his plight.

He had been living like a caged animal. An outcast. Trapped by fear, isolation, emptiness, loneliness, disappointment and self-hatred.

Then his anger turned into terror, and once again I felt the sheer panic of losing music— the most precious thing he and I had ever wanted in life. I hurt badly and increased my grip on him.

Our bodies trembled with rage and quaked until our entire being shattered.

We tilted our head back and screamed like a mortally wounded animal desperate to survive.

Together, we let out a long, hard cry of anguish with all our might.

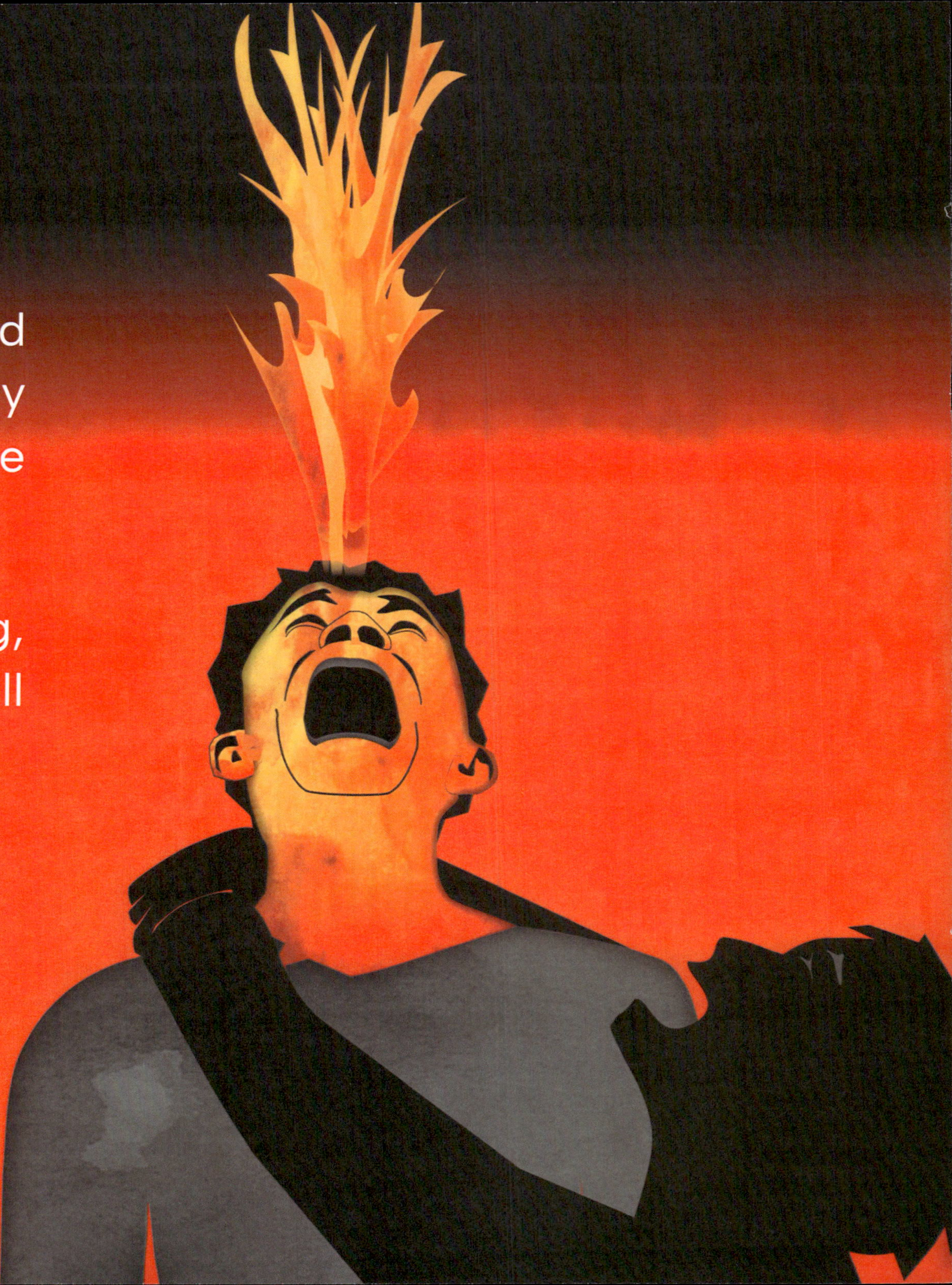

Our chests, my chest, heaved and felt like it would burst. I wanted it to burst. I wanted to be uncaged, even if it meant death.

I wanted to die.

My face became molten. Muscles stretched by my screams until they tore. My throat, a blast furnace. My chest, an inferno.

And then,
in an instant,
our screams
stopped.

We clung to each other in silence.

At that moment, the soul that was my young life was finally, finally, acknowledged and heard.

Heard, held and forgiven.

Held and forgiven.

Held, loved, and forgiven.

Our bodies slowly relaxed.

Exhausted.

The fires in our body cooled in the silence, a blessed release. Frankie and I stood embracing, motionless and silent.

It was then that I knew what to say and do.

I called to my allies to join me in a circle around Frankie, and we held hands.

"Frankie," I said. "This is Leila. She makes me whole because she is part of me. She is part of you, too. And you are part of us."

Next, I introduced Frankie to the Spirit Helpers I had come to know and trust, starting with Teacher, then White Wolf, then Sacred Tree.

Then, spontaneously, something beautiful and remarkable happened.

Other spirits I didn't know began circling around us, each with its own gift of healing. Frankie levitated gently toward the heavens.

Our circle blossomed like a flower, petals fanning upward and outward high above the Garden's treetops. We spoke to him in a single, compassionate voice again and again.

"Frankie, you are whole. You are free. Frankie, you are safe, cared for, and loved."

Frankie continued to rise until he settled some distance above us, floating on his back, free from the very concept of confinement.

At peace.

Healing.

I floated with my spirit friends, immersed in blessed silence. I felt a huge release as my entire Garden became filled with gentle peace.

And gently, my journey came to an end.

I visited my Garden every day after that. Each time, Teacher and I would see Frankie floating high above the Garden floor.

Blissful and safe.

After some time, Coach suggested I invite Frankie to come down from the clouds and into my heart.

And he did so…
quietly…
contentedly…

Coach had guided me and Teacher had taught me well.

Frankie is not angry with me. I am not angry with myself. He is again creating, which I hope is evidenced by the illustrations in this book. Maybe someday, he will make music.

I had released Frankie from his prison at last, and I understood it wasn't Frankie's job to forgive himself. Only I could forgive him. As adult Frank, 63 years old and counting, it was my job to love him and show him compassion. By doing so, I discovered compassion, forgiveness, and loving kindness growing within me for the man that Frankie grew up to be.

HOMECOMING

It's been a year since Leila and Frankie re-entered my life. Each day, benefit from Leila's joy of life and Frankie's freedom. It is true that emotional wellness and healing are not like flipping a switch. It's a process. A Journey. Pun intended.

But now when I have difficult moments, I just remember how Frankie looked, floating blissfully free of pain and confinement, high above the Garden floor, and then I feel Frankie and Leila living and expressing themselves happily in my heart. They both call it home.

And, technically, you cannot be a
burglar in your own home.

MEET COACH

Now it's your turn. Meet Coach.

After walking with Frank through his story of healing and self-discovery, you may find yourself wondering: *What about me?*

If reading *Finally ME* awakened something inside you—a desire to reclaim the parts of yourself that went quiet long ago, or to live with the same sense of truth and freedom you felt between these pages—then perhaps this is where your own journey begins.

As a transformational healer, coach, and shamanic counselor, I guide people who are ready to move beyond anxiety, self-doubt, and the wounds that have kept them small, yet aren't sure how to cross the threshold into the life that's calling them next.

Our work together is a guided return to your own wisdom—through intention, presence, and deep listening to what your body and soul already know. Healing doesn't have to be harsh or heroic; it can unfold gently, with curiosity and compassion.

If you're ready to begin your own journey home, I invite you to reach out.

Visit sound-living.com/meetcoach

I'm excited to help you find your way home to you!

Warmly,

Valerie Devi

ABOUT THE AUTHORS

FRANK SALA is the founder of Cat Gate Graphics [www.catgategraphics.com]. He lives in the Green Mountains of southern Vermont, where he devotes his time to his three main passions—graphic design, gardening, and caring for the cats and kittens at the Second Chance Animal Center in Arlington.

After surviving both a heart attack and stroke, Frank found himself embarking on a journey to heal the early trauma underlying both of those conditions. With his verbal communication temporarily impaired, his expression burst forth in the flowing images of fantasy, emotion, pain, horror, and deliverance that eventually become *Finally ME*.

Frank has three graphic novels in the works. *Emily Has a Beautiful Garden* explores the plight of a woman facing devastating loss who discovers boundless joy from very unexpected sources, while *The Sound Healer* recounts the life of a man who could not stop singing to himself as a child, and explores the healing power of sound, and the sometimes tragically errant nature of memory. His latest, *The Porcupine and the Balloon*, is a children's story about seeking for and finding love.

Valerie Devi Carpenter is a transformational coach, visionary sound healer, and shamanic counselor who helps clients relieve pain, stress, anxiety, and overwhelm, and come home to their calm, steady center. Using pioneering protocols for stress and pain relief, spiritual awakening, and trauma recovery, she guides individuals toward the confidence that allows them to be truly seen and heard. Valerie's mission is to help people find happiness in their work and relationships, while replenishing the vital energy they need to work, play, sleep, and love.

Valerie's forty-year career in the performing arts inspired her to create a signature program that has helped hundreds of clients free their powerful voice for self-healing, spiritual growth, and to speak up for what they want—and get it!

She is the founder of Valerie Devi Sound Living [www.sound-living.com] in the San Francisco Bay Area. She holds professional certifications in sound healing, integrative medicine, and neuro-psychoacoustics from the California Institute of Integral Studies, the Acutonics Institute of Integrative Medicine, Integrated Listening Systems, Advanced Brain Technologies, the Vox Mundi School of the Voice, and The Awakened School. Valerie is co-author of *Free Your Voice: Awaken to Life Through Singing* and her upcoming memoir, *The Sound of Self.*

ACKNOWLEDGEMENTS

This book has been a labor of love, healing, and discovery—and neither of us could have walked this path alone.

From Frank:

To Valerie—thank you for standing by me through the darkest chapters and witnessing me into the light. Your compassion, insight, and fierce belief in my healing changed my life. To the spirits who showed up in the journeys—especially White Wolf, my sacred Tree, and the Guides who helped me retrieve what was lost—I will never forget you. And to my family, friends, and community—thank you for your support, patience, and love.

From Valerie:

Frank, it's been the deepest honor to walk beside you, both as your guide and your creative partner. Your courage, artistry, and willingness to go all in have inspired me more than you know. To my beloved community of clients, teachers, and fellow travelers—thank you for reminding me again and again why this work matters. And to my own spiritual allies, thank you for keeping the channel clear and my heart open.

From both of us:
To Stacey Smekofske and her InPrint Academy—thank you for demystifying the publishing path and patiently guiding us from screen to shelf.

To Tara Mayberry of Teaberry Creative—your thoughtful eye and steady hand turned our words and images into a beautiful book. We would have been lost without you both.

To Jill and Hank—who appear in these pages with such love and presence—you are forever in our hearts.

And to you, dear reader, thank you for showing up. May this book meet you right where you are and help you come home to who you've always been.

BOOK CLUB & REFLECTION QUESTIONS

This book invites deep contemplation, making it a beautiful choice for personal reflection or group discussion. Here are a few prompts to get you started:

- What part of Frank's story resonated with you the most—and why?
- Have you ever felt like a "burglar in your own body"? What might your version of wholeness look like?
- Frank meets powerful allies in the spirit world. Who or what feels like an ally in your own life?
- What part of yourself have you exiled—and are ready to welcome back?
- The book explores what it means to come home to yourself. Where in your own life are you being invited "home"?
- Which moment in *Finally ME* stirred something in you—a memory, a longing, or a question about your own path
- Frank's healing journey began with the courage to face what he'd avoided. What truth or emotion in your own story is asking to be witnessed with compassion?
- Are there places in your own journey where you could use support or guidance? What might that support look like or feel like for you?

RESOURCES

For copyright inquiries or permission to reprint, please contact Valerie: valerie@sound-living.com

Learn more about Valerie Devi Sound Living, www.sound-living.com/meetcoach

For graphic design, please contact Frank: catgategraphics@gmail.com

To learn more about the Sacred Garden, check out: Hank Wesselman, Ph.D *The Journey to the Sacred Garden: A Guide to Traveling in the Spiritual Realms* (Carlsbad, CA: Hay House, Inc., 2003)

Sound Living Wisdom

www.ingramcontent.com/pod-product-compliance
Lightning Source LLC
LaVergne TN
LVRC080922210926
848486LV00015B/399

* 9 7 9 8 9 9 0 2 5 4 7 0 1 *